# THE
# DRAMATIC
# CONCEPTS OF
# ANTONIN
# ARTAUD

# THE

# DRAMATIC

# CONCEPTS OF

# ANTONIN

# ARTAUD

by Eric Sellin

The University of Chicago Press

CHICAGO AND LONDON

Library of Congress Catalog Card Number: 74–21345

THE UNIVERSITY OF CHICAGO PRESS, CHICAGO 60637
The University of Chicago Press, Ltd., London
© 1968, 1975 by The University of Chicago. All rights
reserved. Published 1968. Second Impression 1975
Printed in the United States of America
ISBN: 0–226–74784–0 (clothbound) ; 0–226–74785–9 (paperbound)

# Preface

This book is geared for the theater-minded individual, whether or not he is a French linguist, and I have, therefore, translated all French passages into English. However, the book will no doubt be read by many already familiar with the works of Artaud, and for them to find some titles only in translation would be irksome and confusing. I have, therefore, used my judgment in the rendering of titles. For example, I have not translated titles of periodicals; I have given titles of works by Artaud and other French-speaking authors in translation with the original in parentheses on first occurrence, otherwise only in English; I have not translated titles if doing so would be merely anglicizing or repeating a name as in *Huon de Bordeaux* or *Gigogne;* and I have used English titles for works by non-French authors, such as Strindberg. The bibliography and notes retain the original French titles, of course; and the index provides a main entry in English, with a cross reference from the French title.

When it was decided that the French should be translated into idiomatic English, it no longer seemed necessary to use ellipses and brackets quite so meticulously, or to observe capitalization in a sentence in which the quotation pursues without interruption the sense of my own phrase, but I have scrupulously observed these conventions when the text is from an

English source. I have made minor adjustments throughout, however, in order to make the style of this book uniform in the matter of capitalization of titles, placement of punctuation in relation to quotation marks, and so forth.

Translation presented a number of problems in that I wished to retain the precise original content and intent and yet did not wish to clutter the text with parenthetical material from the original. I have coped with the problems in three ways, and it is important that the reader know the extent of my license and fully understand that for any further study of specific sections of Artaud's writings he ought to go to the originals which are, in most cases, readily available. Most problems in translation naturally arose over words or phrases which either had no English equivalent or which had several possible translations because they were general, ambiguous, or paradoxical. The problems were dealt with in the following ways: (1) a few words or expressions, such as "metteur en scène," and its derivative, "mise en scène," have been retained in the original, not italicized, since they cannot readily be rendered by such words as "director" and "stage design" and have been here adopted as parallels to anglicized words like "entrepreneur"; (2) some words, such as "matériellement" and "principe," which have several equivalents in English but whose intended usage seems clear in a given context, have been translated according to my judgment, and where the ambiguity is pertinent I have either used two words for one or added the original word or words in parentheses, as in the case of an untranslatable pun; and (3) some words or expressions, such as "théâtre digestif," which have no adequate equivalents and at the same time should be clear to someone knowing little or no French, have been left in the original within quotation marks. I have left the names of actual theaters in the original, be they buildings or organizations, but have referred to conceptualized theaters in English. Thus, Artaud's essay "The

Theater of Cruelty" ("Le Théâtre de la cruauté") is an explanation of his idea of a Theater of Cruelty, which he attempted
to manifest in 1935 when he founded his Théâtre de la
Cruauté in order to stage *The Cenci* at the Théâtre des Folies-
Wagram.

My constant goal has been to achieve an interesting and
undistracting style and organization without suppressing pertinent facts or difficult forays into the conceptual realm. To this
end, I have relegated all notes to the back of the book save a
few which are only meaningful as elaborations of the text and
which have, therefore, been placed at the foot of the page.
However, the notes at the end of the book are not merely
documentary and often contain interesting and detailed bio-
bibliographical, comparative, and analytical comment, but
they need only be examined by the reader who wishes to take a
second look after he has read the entire work or by the scholar
or critic who is engaged in research.

Finally, I have had to be selective. My plan was to get to the
heart of the subject by means of a thorough examination of
major cultural areas and works of art, and while I hope there
are no oversights, there are some inevitable omissions. Two
conspicuous areas I have not discussed in any depth—
Artaud's influence and Artaud and the cinema—since they fall
outside the scope of my intent and present specific justifica-
tions for exclusion as well.

The influence of Artaud on playwrights and directors is at
once so widespread and so vague as to be inestimable save in a
separate study which would establish its own critical norms;
and even then the relative degree of influence and coincidence
would be difficult to establish, much more so than is the
influence of others upon Artaud, which I have explored in the
first part of this study. It is simply much easier to determine
the reception on a given receiver than it is to determine, on the
basis of a transmitter, how many receivers have picked up

signals. This problem is compounded by the fact that in intellectual and cultural matters the signals of an age can greatly resemble those given off by any one man who is of his time or a man from an earlier period who was ahead of his time. Let me give one example of the problems involved that made me decide to omit altogether any attempt to trace in a methodical manner the impact of Artaud on modern theater. Beckett, Ionesco, and Genet are frequently referred to as having been influenced by Artaud or having implemented his ideas on the stage. In answer to queries, Beckett denied having been influenced by Artaud or being familiar with his ideas; Ionesco denied any connection except certain coincidental preoccupations and the fact that he had read Artaud's essays without much interest a number of years earlier; and Roger Blin has stated that Genet was not influenced by Artaud nor had he read his works.[1] Conversely, Adamov, who readily admits to Artaud's direct influence on the development of his concept of the exploitation of stage space, does far less than the other three to implement what one could call an Artaudian mise en scène. Add to this the fact that secondary and tertiary "influencees" like Peter Brook and his disciples have popularized a misinterpretation of Artaud's ideas based to a large extent on a semantic rather than metaphysical or aesthetic understanding of the word "cruelty" and it becomes evident that we cannot begin to answer the questions that arise: Was X influenced by Artaud? Did he know it? Although he claims to have been, was he significantly influenced? Was he influenced less by Artaud's ideas than by Director Y's adoption of Director Z's misreading of Artaud?

As for the other omission—cinema—Artaud became disenchanted with films on the advent of sound and, no doubt, because—despite some brilliant interpretations—he was repeatedly shunted into minor roles. It is true that he brought to film scenarios many of the aesthetic and philosophical attitudes he held with regard to theater, and in this measure my discussion of the dramatic concepts will be revelatory in connection with his cinematographic undertakings. However, since Artaud himself did not consider theater and cinema either inseparable or of equal importance, I have only cursorily considered this area and have left its full investigation to others; and, although there are several fine articles on the subject of Artaud and the cinema, there is certainly room for further study in that direction. My work is neither a biography—though I have provided a biographical introduction—nor an exhaustive the-man-and-his-works type of volume, and I have limited myself, as is fitting, to the subject of my study. The reader who becomes interested in Artaud finds himself implicated in a many-faceted world, and, indeed, it required great self-restraint for me to limit myself to Artaud's dramatic concepts, in view of the incandescence of some of the extraordinary poems he wrote toward the end of his life. They are messages from the other side of reality and remind us of the tortured souls of whom Artaud speaks who are seen making signs through the flames as they burn at the stake.

Artaud was a visionary and, as such, he functioned on the frontier of definition. The visionary sees beyond the words he is condemned to use in his effort to express his vision; and this state of affairs brings with it a problem of critical methodology. One can restrict oneself to the ponderables or one can attempt to define a critical framework in keeping with the metaphysical problems to be considered. I have depended on ponderables and documented fact wherever possible, but I felt compelled as well to explore Artaud's ideas not only as concept but also as vision. Therefore, from a wide and repeated reading of Artaud's works, I created a critical definition that may have some weaknesses but which I feel is essentially sound and will facilitate the discussion of Artaud's ideas. Thus, I deduced a definition which I then set about applying inductively. If at first it appears that I have injected a great deal of myself into a subjective definition seemingly unrelated to Artaud, let me assure the reader that in order to derive this definition I first subjected myself to Artaud's ideas, and then based the definition on the many truths, ponderable and visionary, that I found in them. Without first establishing critical premises and vectors—even if sometimes they are established in reference to themselves in a "closed circuit"—I should have been able only to paraphrase, to quote, and to lose myself in the maze of paradox and contradiction in which Artaud frequently moved intellectually. Whereas the Euro-American strives for unity, in many primitive societies the idea of paradox, opposition, and contradiction is not only tolerated but is actually held essential for a continuing vitality in the society.[2] Instead of trying to unify Artaud's highly fragmented and paradoxical thought processes, I have rather based my definition on the concept of duality and recognized the enlightening power of paradox.

According to Diderot, on the stage the true is "the conformity of actions, speech, facial expression, voice, movement, and gesture with an ideal model imagined by the poet."[3] Diderot's remark remains as valid for our time as it was for his, because the poet's imagined ideal model will change with the times and be conditioned by those times, as will the poet. Thus, although some critics—for example, Robert Brustein in *The Theater of Revolt*—would relate all superior modern drama to revolt, the *avant-garde* is not a unilateral revolt, for the poet's imagined model had to find its genesis in the antithetical environment of the period in which he flourished. What was meant by the concept of voice, gesture, and so forth, in the time of Diderot would be determined by the poet and the model to which he wished the theatrical ingredients to conform. And this principle will obtain in any period, ancient or modern.

In this study I have attempted to reveal Artaud's imagined ideal model, and the degree to which he was successful in approximating that model. To do this, I have undertaken (1) an examination of those areas of drama and culture that played an important role in the genesis of Artaud's dramatic ideas; (2) an exegesis of the ideas; and (3) a consideration of Artaud's own efforts to implement those ideas in his dramaturgy.

I should like to thank the following people: MM. Dannie Abse, Arthur Adamov, Samuel Beckett, Denys-Paul Bouloc, Eugène Ionesco, Jean Rousselot, and Mme Claire Goll, all of whom kindly responded to queries; Mme Paule Thévenin, who selflessly and patiently shared her detailed bio-bibliographical knowledge of Artaud; Professors Robert K. Bishop, Bruce Morrissette, and Eric Bentley, who read this book in manuscript and made helpful suggestions; Professor William Roach, whose repeated and always timely help was subtle but crucial; and Birgitta, who in the hard years showed a rare faith.

# Acknowledgments

I wish to thank Editions Gallimard, Coward-McCann, Inc., and Calder and Boyars, Ltd. for permission to translate and use quotations from Artaud's *Œuvres complètes* (copyright Editions Gallimard 1956, 1961, 1964, 1966, 1967); Marc Barbezat of L'Arbalète for permission to translate and use quotations from *Les Tarahumaras;* the Musée du Louvre for permission to reproduce Lucas van Leyden's painting, *Lot and His Daughters;* and the Peabody Museum for permission to reproduce the detail from the Codex Nuttall.

# Preface to Phoenix Edition

Many articles and book chapters about Artaud have appeared since 1968, and we should in this context mention the names of Jacques Derrida, Henri Béhar, Mary Ann Caws, J. H. Matthews, Maurice LaBelle, Franco Tonelli, and Ruby Cohn, to name but a few. Some book-length studies on Artaud have come out, of which the following deserve particular attention: *Artaud,* papers by Philippe Sollers and others, "Collection 10/18" (Paris: Union Générale d'Editions, 1973); Jean-Louis Brau, *Antonin Artaud* (Paris: Table Ronde, 1971); Naomi Greene, *Antonin Artaud, Poet without Words* (New York: Simon and Schuster, 1970); Daniel Joski, *Artaud* (Paris: Editions Universitaires, 1970); Bettina Knapp, *Antonin Artaud, Man of Vision* (New York: David Lewis, 1969); Franco Tonelli, *L'Esthétique de la cruauté, Etudes des implications esthétiques du "Théâtre de la Cruauté" d'Antonin Artaud* (Paris: Nizet, 1972); Alain Virmaux, *Antonin Artaud et le théâtre* (Paris: Seghers, 1970).

Editions of the *Œuvres complètes* slowly approach completion. The separate publication of Artaud's *Lettres à Génica Athanasiou* (Paris: Gallimard, 1969) and the notes accompanying recent volumes of the *Œuvres complètes* provide new insight into Artaud's private life. A considerable amount of Artaud material is now available in English translation with the publication of: Antonin Artaud, *Collected Works*, 3 vols., translated by V. Corti (London: Calder and Boyars, I [1968], II [1971], III [1972]); Antonin Artaud, *The Cenci*, translated by S. Watson-Taylor (London: Caldar and Boyars, 1969; New York: Grove Press, 1970); and *Selected Writings of Antonin Artaud*, edited by S. Sontag, translated by H. Weaver (New York: Farrar, Straus and Giroux, scheduled for 1975).

There has been some good work in much-neglected areas of Artaudiana, but I feel that *The Dramatic Concepts of Antonin Artaud* has not been superseded by any of the new scholarship. Perhaps this is because, when writing the book, I relied heavily on what Artaud actually said and did and resisted the temptation to rhapsodize, to mythify, or to use Artaud as a "psycho-reflective" agent to demonstrate preconceived ideas. I feel that what I have said in this study not only remains absolutely valid today but needs, in fact, to be reaffirmed more than ever. Artaud, as a real man and a real force, has been progressively ignored, yielding rather to a "notion" to which well-wishers have given the name Artaud, a notion which is every year more removed from the realities of the man's life and the special virtues of his real contribution to the history of literature and dramatic theory.

E.S., 1974

# Contents

# Introduction

Antonin Artaud was born in Marseilles on September 4, 1896, at 8 A.M.[1] His father was French and his mother was from a family of Greek origin settled in Smyrna. When he was fourteen years old, Artaud and several friends founded a little magazine in which Artaud published his first poems under the pseudonym Louis des Attides. These early poems reveal the influence of Baudelaire and Poe.

In 1915 Artaud experienced the first physical pains caused by his mental disturbances and went to the first of the many sanitariums he was to stay in during much of his lifetime. He was mobilized and sent to Digne in 1916, but given a medical discharge nine months later.

After a succession of visits to a number of sanitariums, he was moved to Chanet near Neuchâtel in Switzerland, where he stayed under the care of a Dr. Dardel for nearly two years. While there he was encouraged to pursue his new interest in drawing. He was then sent, after a brief stay in Marseilles, to Paris to be under the care of a Dr. Toulouse at Villejuif. Dr. and Mme Toulouse encouraged Artaud's literary efforts, and Dr. Toulouse made him secretary of his little review, *Demain*, in which Artaud published some of his own poems. He also

1

edited and wrote the preface for a collection of Dr. Toulouse's writings.

In 1923 Artaud sent a group of poems to the *Nouvelle Revue Française*. The poems were traditional in style, with overtones of Baudelaire, Poe, Corbière, and Laforgue. Jacques Rivière turned them down but expressed a desire to meet the young poet and invited him to call on him, which Artaud did on June 5, 1923.

A very probing correspondence ensued concerning the "recevabilité" of Artaud's poems for publication, and about critical appreciation in general. Artaud's letters are composed in terms of confession, contrition, and rationalization. He wrote, "the few things I have sent to you constitute the fragments I have succeeded in saving from total oblivion," [2] and added that he suffered from "a dreadful illness of the mind." [3] It is one of those ironies of fate that Jacques Rivière was steadfast in his rejection of Artaud's poems but was so fascinated by the letters* that he published them in 1924. Such ironies were to pursue Artaud throughout his career and even after his death.

When Artaud came to Paris in 1920 he met Lugné-Poe who gave him a bit part in Henri de Régnier's *Sganarelle's Scruples* (*Les Scrupules de Sganarelle*). In 1921 he attracted the attention of the famous actor Firmin Gémier who referred him to Charles Dullin.

Artaud played a number of roles in the next several years, first with Dullin at the Théâtre de l'Atelier and then with the Pitoëff troupe. While with Dullin he played a variety of parts, including a Moorish king in Alexandre Arnoux's *Mariana and Galoan* (*Mariana et Galoan*), Anselme in Molière's *The Miser* (*L'Avare*), Pedro Urdemala in Jacinto Grau's *Mr. Pygmalion*, Charlemagne in Arnoux's *Huon de Bordeaux*, and he not only

---

* "One thing strikes me: the contrast between the extraordinary precision of your self-diagnosis and the vagueness or, at least, the formlessness of the renditions you have attempted." [4]

2

gave one of his best performances as Basilio in Calderón's *Life Is a Dream*, but designed the costumes and sets for the play as well.

With Georges and Ludmilla Pitoëff's troupe, Artaud brilliantly interpreted the minor role of one of the two Heavenly Policemen in Ferenc Molnar's *Liliom* in the last production of the Pitoëffs' 1922–23 season at the Comédie des Champs-Elysées; and the following season he acted in several plays, including *The Little Hut* by Alexander Blok, Pirandello's *Six Characters in Search of an Author*, and Andreev's *He Who Gets Slapped*. He also acted in Karel Čapek's *R.U.R.* and in film clips incorporated into Yvan Goll's play *Mathusalem* in 1924.

Artaud's activity was not limited to the legitimate stage. He was also interested in the cinema and was quite active in films, as an actor and as an aspiring scenarist, from 1922 to 1935. His most memorable roles were Marat in *Napoleon* (Abel Gance, 1926) and the confessor-monk Massieu in *The Passion of Joan of Arc* (Carl Dreyer, 1928). Artaud's scenarios of this period included *The Shell and the Clergyman* (*La Coquille et le clergyman*), which was the only scenario by Artaud ever produced. It was written in 1927 and first shown on February 18, 1928, at a tempestuous *première* at the Ursulines, during which Artaud insulted the producer, Germaine Dulac, with whom he had disagreed over her interpretation. Despite its shortcomings, the film contained many new ideas and, as Ado Kyrou has said, "historically *The Shell and the Clergyman* was the first surrealist film, owing nothing to the practices of *pure* cinema." [5]

In the mid-twenties Artaud was already dreaming of founding a theater of his own. After his brief association with the surrealists, the culminating moment of which was his composition of nearly the entire third number of *La Révolution Surréaliste*, Artaud broke with Breton, and late in 1926 he began to plan the Théâtre Alfred Jarry with Roger Vitrac and Robert Aron. The first manifesto for the new theater appeared in the November 1, 1926, issue of the *Nouvelle Revue Française*, and on December 12, Mme Allendy, who with her husband, the psychiatrist, had befriended Artaud, drafted a circular letter soliciting financial aid.

Although by April, 1927, only some three thousand francs had been collected and turned over to Robert Aron, the three metteurs en scène decided to attempt a production. In May, rehearsals for Vitrac's *The Mysteries of Love* (*Les Mystères de l'amour*) were begun in a rehearsal room which Dullin had made available to them.

On June 1 and 2, 1927, two evening performances were presented by the Théâtre Alfred Jarry on the stage of the Théâtre de Grenelle which had been rented for the occasion. The program consisted of one drama by each of the three directors: *Burnt Belly: or, The Crazy Mother* (*Ventre brûlé ou la mère folle*) by Artaud, *The Mysteries of Love* by Vitrac, and *Gigogne* by Robert Aron, which was presented under the pseudonym, Max Robur.

The theater presented three more productions in 1928 and 1929 before it was finally discontinued. The productions were: (1) an act from *Break of Noon* (*Le Partage de midi*) by Paul Claudel, given "against the author's wishes," plus Pudovkin's revolutionary film, *Mother*, adapted from Gorky, presented at a matinee on January 14, 1928, at the Comédie des Champs-Elysées; (2) *A Dream Play* by Strindberg, presented at matinees on June 2 and 9, 1928, at the Théâtre de l'Avenue; and (3) *Victor: or, The Children Take Power* (*Victor ou les enfants au pouvoir*) by Roger Vitrac, presented at matinees on December 24 and 29, 1928, and January 5, 1929, at the Comédie des Champs-Elysées.[6]

Artaud then tried on various occasions to associate himself with Louis Jouvet, Charles Dullin, and others, usually as an assistant director, with the ultimate hope of gaining some autonomy within their stable organizations, but these efforts were unsuccessful. His only subsequent attempt to found a theater occurred when he established the Théâtre de la Cruauté and put on one play, *The Cenci* (*Les Cenci*), adapted by Artaud from Stendhal and Shelley, which had its *première* on May 6, 1935, at the Théâtre des Folies-Wagram and ran for seventeen days.[7] Disappointment over *The Cenci*, which was indifferently received, brought a turning-point in Artaud's personal life.

In January, 1936, Artaud sailed for Mexico, where he hoped to locate an authentic primitive culture among whose people he might find preserved a mystical urgency in the relationship between life and art. Arriving in Mexico City in February after a brief stay in Havana, Artaud had no money, and to survive he borrowed from friends in France, gave a number of lectures, and wrote some articles for *El Nacional*. After visiting the museums, he made a trip into the interior, where he visited the Tarahumara Indians and witnessed some of their rituals. Artaud believed that during this trip he was placed under a spell by an agent of the "international dark forces." In November, 1936, he returned to France, and in the ensuing months was reconciled with André Breton.

In August, 1937, Artaud went to Ireland and the Aran Islands, ostensibly to return to its rightful place a cane which he had acquired and which he claimed had belonged to St. Patrick. However, he was no doubt urged to go there as well by an impulse akin to that which had prompted the Mexican trip, that is, in search of a primal theater.

Artaud's full itinerary is not known, but he landed at Cobh on August 14, 1937, and was in Kilronan on Inishmore, the largest of the Aran Islands, by August 23. He spent most of September in Dublin, still in possession of the cane. At the end of September, after several public incidents, he was arrested

5

by the Irish police. As the French consulate in Dublin informed Jean Paulhan, "M. Artaud's presence in Dublin was pointed out to the legation toward the end of last September by the Irish police. They expressed a desire to repatriate our fellow countryman, who was without resources and manifested a high degree of overexcitement. M. Artaud, on whose behalf the legation intervened in every manner possible, boarded the *Washington* at Cobh on September 29 and must have arrived at Le Havre the next day." [8] Upon arrival in Le Havre, Artaud, who had been confined to a strait jacket after an incident aboard the *Washington,* was sent to the Quatremarre sanitarium.

Artaud spent the next nine years in mental institutions, during which time his most important theoretical essays, composed in the early thirties, were collected under the title *The Theater and Its Double* (*Le Théâtre et son double*) and published by Gallimard in its "Collection Métamorphoses" in 1938. After Le Havre came Sotteville-les-Rouen, Sainte-Anne, and Ville-Evrard, where the conditions were ghastly. In 1943 Robert Desnos and several other friends succeeded in getting Artaud transferred to the asylum at Rodez in southern France, where Artaud fell under the care of Dr. Ferdière who administered Artaud's much-discussed electric shock treatments. While at Rodez, Artaud began to write and draw again and showed sufficient signs of remission for Dr. Ferdière, who had been approached by Arthur Adamov and other friends of Artaud, to agree to sign the poet's release if assured that Artaud could provide for himself.

In May, 1946, Artaud came to Paris. A considerable sum of money was raised by holding a sale of manuscripts and drawings at the Galerie Pierre on June 17, 1946, and a gala evening of famous actors reading from Artaud's poems at the Théâtre Sarah-Bernhardt on June 7, 1946. The once handsome Artaud, now a cadaverous, toothless wraith, settled in a small stone cottage on the grounds of the sanitarium at Ivry where, though not committed, he could be under the care and observation of Dr. Delmas.

Artaud gradually resumed his interest in the theater, which he had abandoned after *The Cenci,* but he never staged another play. In January, 1947, he gave a lecture or "Tête-à-tête," which was a sensation, at the Vieux-Colombier; and in November, 1947, Artaud and several other actors recorded for the radio his piece entitled *To Have Done with the Judgment of God (Pour en finir avec le jugement de Dieu)*, but it was never broadcast.

Artaud's body was ravaged by cancer, and he began to take ever-increasing doses of chloral and laudanum to allay his suffering. On March 4, 1948, the gardener of the sanitarium who brought Artaud his breakfast every morning found him dead, seated at the foot of his bed. The day before his death he had composed a note on legal paper making Paule Thévenin executor of his manuscripts. She has recently written that, after all these years, she has "arrived at this conclusion: Antonin Artaud died exactly as he wanted and probably when he wanted." [9]

# Part One

## ANTECEDENTS

# Solar and Lunar Drama: A Definition

The plays and rituals that most interested Antonin Artaud fall roughly into two categories whose general nature has led me to adopt for expediency a binary definition of solar and lunar drama. I shall call solar drama that which is characterized by action, the Male, revolt, and self-assertion; and I shall call lunar drama that which is characterized by stasis, the Female, acquiescence, and self-abnegation. Artaud admired plays from both categories, but in his theoretical writings he tended to favor solar drama. I shall, in this part of the study, consider the solar and lunar dramas that most affected Artaud, and thereby attempt to determine his "imagined ideal." However, let us first consider briefly the general characteristics of each type of drama.

Solar drama takes a number of forms, but it inevitably entails a gesture of defiance or cruelty of some magnitude. An

11

eruption of evil is not necessary to revolt but frequently accompanies it. Thus the act of defying the gods is not evil, save from the prejudiced viewpoint of the priests and practitioners of the particular religion, but the implementation of that rebellion in murder we may universally call evil. Thus Atreus, to stride among the stars, must kill his brother's children; but if one is concerned with dramatic rebellion on the metaphysical level, the gesture must be evaluated metaphysically and not psychologically, and certainly not socially, for to do this is to lay down social laws for art at the expense of the aesthetic laws that properly determine it.

The two great forms of metaphysical defiance in modern drama are the attempted overthrow of the gods and the gratuitous act.* The gratuitous act is executed without regard for societal conventions, and it therefore often tends to be evil, criminal, and immoral from normal society's viewpoint. The gesture of attempted overthrow of the gods constitutes in many respects what Robert Brustein calls messianic revolt and is, in our day, the outgrowth of Nietzsche's precepts, the romantic rebellion, and the will of the poet to play the messiah and transmit dreams from the cosmos.

I should like to examine for a moment the gesture of rebellion that does not attempt to destroy God but, because it embraces the cause of God's enemy, is described in terms of Satan's own values. The binary standard of two parallel ethics permits the man who elevates himself to the top in the one ethic to defy by his very existence the supremacy of the godhead of the other ethic. Dualism was germane to the early animistic stages of civilization; and the soterial questions which presumably arose, as Freud has suggested, from the contemplation of death and the rapid metamorphosis that ac-

---

* Gide's exploration of the gratuitous act is relevant, but I am using the term in the simple sense of an act that has no motive or is at most self-rewarding.

companies it, were answered in various ways and forms according to each particular society; but the answer inevitably contained somewhere at its core the concept of dualism: between good and evil or between benevolent and malevolent taboos. Naturally man strives to do good and to placate whatever benevolent or malevolent force he believes in, with an eye to leading a good and a safe life, but implicit in good and its observance is the antithetical concept of the observance of evil, for, as some interpret it, Ahriman was created as a by-product of Ormazd in a moment of doubt on the part of the latter, and thus inheres in his realm and very conscience. Similarly, the whole is a balance between the *yin* and the *yang* in Taoism. Thus, he who pays obeisance to Ormazd or Jehovah must also reckon with Ahriman or Lucifer,* just as he who has touched a taboo king can only be saved by the intentionally curative application of that king's touch or that of a man of equally powerful taboo or mana.[2]

The balance between evil and good wavers according to the doctrine and the individual. Mazdaism, Manicheism, and certain Christian heresies lend different weights to the side of evil. The men who carried on the tradition of Baal and Ahriman differed in the degree of their commitment to evil, but they all tended to investigate and portray the violent, the hideous, the brutal, and the destructive. As André Breton writes, paraphrasing Léon Pierre-Quint, since evil is, for writers in this tradition, "the form in which the driving force of historical development presents itself, it is meet to stress its justification, which cannot be more readily done than by bas-

---

* It is this concept combined with that of predestination that gave rise to such heretical groups as the Iscariots, who considered that Judas' betrayal was necessary to the consummation of Christ's martyrdom and the redemption of mankind, and that, if predestination is a fact, God himself used Iscariot to achieve his aims. For the same reasons the Ophites worshiped the serpent as it provided them with the knowledge necessary to combat their enemy and creator Iadalbaoth.[1]

13

ing it on forbidden desires inherent in primitive sexual activity and particularly as manifested in sadism." [3] In the late nineteenth century, and the twentieth, we have found increasing critical and public acceptance of, and even admiration for, the demonic in writing, dramaturgy, and painting. In the last hundred-odd years since the 1857 suppression of half a dozen poems of Baudelaire's *Flowers of Evil* (*Les Fleurs du mal*), many concessions have been made to works of art reflecting violence, forbidden sexual themes, and madness—most of the concessions occurring critically in the last fifty years and publicly in the last fifteen or twenty.

Lunar drama is characterized by the misty, the mysterious, and by darkness; by symbolism of the sort found in the theater of Maeterlinck and Synge; and by the futility and stagnation characterized by the nocturnal plays of Samuel Beckett. Whereas solar drama is composed of light, action, and outburst, lunar drama is composed of darkness, stillness, and silence.

The lunar drama of the period prior to and coincidental with Artaud's years of conceptualizing, which created the climate in which he formulated his ideas, is characterized by inaction or acquiescence and illustrates the precept that a conventional plot or narrative is concrete and psychological whereas lunar drama strives to portray a state of mind that is symbolic and metaphysical. Its dramatists rejected the metaphysics and aesthetics of action for those of thought, spirit, and rhythm.

This rhythm tends to take two particular forms: the fluid, implacable, seemingly predestined rhythm of Chekhov, Maeterlinck, and Synge; and the contrapuntal rhythm of the episodic plays of Büchner (*Woyzeck*), Strindberg (*The Ghost Sonata*), Brecht (*Baal*), Apollinaire (*The Breasts of Tiresias* [*Les Mamelles de Tirésias*]), and Vitrac (*Victor*). Even in episodic plays there is a thread, theme, or rhythm running through them that ties together the incidents, and that rhythm is what characterizes the plays as lunar drama as I have defined it. Thus two plays as disparate as the tragic *Woyzeck* and the grotesque *King Ubu* (*Ubu roi*) are compatible within our definition on the basis of this rhythm. Ubu's gestures of rebellion are not rational and therefore do not constitute an ideal revolt or solar drama, just as a farce like Ionesco's *The Bald Soprano* (*La Cantatrice chauve*) may be considered as belonging to the same family of drama as Beckett's or Arrabal's plays. The clichés in *The Bald Soprano* are dead objects—as are the chairs and the corpse in the same playwright's *The Chairs* (*Les Chaises*) and *Amedeus* (*Amédée*)—the devitalized memories with which man thinks he is reaching out to someone and ultimately to everyone, whereas the clichés, in fact, systematically lay down a barrier between us and the animistic level toward which metaphysical endeavors ought generally to be directed. This devitalized, inert matter of clichés and chairs is, despite the unusual visual articulation on stage, related to the more conventional articulation of *Waiting for Godot* (*En attendant Godot*) or *Endgame* (*Fin de partie*), with their desolation, or to the parabolical clichés of Arrabal's *The Automobile Graveyard* (*Le Cimetière des voitures*). These plays are, despite a number of superficial differences, in the tradition of lunar theater and are in the same stream, as it were, with the drama of Chekhov, Maeterlinck, Büchner, and Strindberg.

# Solar Drama and Artaud

The two greatest influences on Artaud's dramatic theories were ancient Mexican culture and the oriental theater, the one solar, the other lunar. The latter has generally been thought to be the keystone in the structure of Artaud's theoretical writing, but the interest in and research on Mexican culture may date back to as early as 1932–33, or only one or two years after he witnessed the 1931 Balinese dance performance that had such an impact on his ideas.

Artaud went to Mexico in 1936. The trip was undertaken in an effort to find a people whose culture might conform to his preconceptions of a pure culture and in search of a primitive theater that might afford him new dramatic revelations. From Havana he wrote to Jean Paulhan. "Since docking at Havana I have been seeing intellectuals and artists and already I feel I am in the vein I was seeking. I am even wondering if this time the illusions will not prove inferior to the reality." [4]

Artaud was impressed by the numbers of ancient tribes in Mexico, but the germ of his disenchantment with the country in general is reflected in his condemnation of the governmental attitude. If, since the revolution, "the Indian has ceased to be the pariah of Mexico," it is no less true that "they [the government] consider the Indian masses to be uncultured, and the predominant movement in Mexico is 'to raise the uncultured Indians up to an occidental notion of culture, up to the (SINISTER) advantages of civilization.' " [5] The culture that Artaud was seeking was not lost, but it was badly decimated: "This culture subsists, it is in tatters, but it subsists." [6] Artaud went to visit the small ingrown tribe of the Tarahumaras in search of "the heirs of an era when the world still possessed a culture, a culture which was one with life." [7] I should like to consider this culture briefly, and then the codices and rites that reflect it, with which Artaud was familiar.

The various legends of Quetzalcoatl's birth as One, or as the offspring of a primal Pair, indicate an ambivalence in his conception. In either case he is related to the two spheres, for if he is not himself primal he is at least born of the primal god who is Heaven and who has fecundated with his sunbeams and

16

rays the recipient and supine primal goddess Earth, Quetzalcoatl being the air between and appropriately called the wind
god.[8]

No doubt Quetzalcoatl contained elements of the sun and
the moon, the Male and the Female, and he contained the
astronomically founded duality of life and death, rise and
decline, the shedding of the old skin in renewal. Danzel writes
that, "From the standpoint of nature mythology, we may designate Quetzalcoatl as the moon: the waning moon which at
the end of the month dies under the beams of the morning star,
for the moon, like the god's heart seems to turn into the
morning star, that rises just as the moon vanishes." [9] However,
if Quetzalcoatl is the moon in nature mythology, his sacrificial
acts and his upward surge are metaphysically solar. This is
also implied if not substantiated on the symbolic level by the
relationship of Quetzalcoatl to other sacred symbols, such as
the eagle, the plumed serpent, and fire, this last being reminiscent of his own self-consumption in flames and subsequent
phoenix-like rebirth.

I am unable to go deeply here into ancient Mexican symbolism and its pictographic relationship to the metaphysical quest
for oneness or a vital balance of opposites. I should rather like
to stress the aesthetic aspect of the Mexican hierograms from
the viewpoint of action and Gestalt, for it is this side of the
ancient culture that is ponderable and that Artaud could conceivably hope to implement on the stage, and without which he
could not hope to begin to approach a metaphysical theater.
The ceremonies of primary interest to us are the sacrificial rite
and the peyote ritual; and the principal symbols are blood and
the sun, which are intimately connected with these ceremonies.
The actions connected with the ceremonies are solar in the
sense in which we have used that word.

The peyote ritual usually takes place at night,[10] and since
the agent is hallucinogenic, the ritual may be said to relate to

17

death and the phantasmagorical and to have as its aim oblivion; but the gesture, the ritual itself, is solar since it is active and not static, positive and not negative.

Artaud turned to ancient Mexico in search of fulfilment of his ever-growing need for self-realization and the discovery of a theater related to man's quest for the *pneuma*. He frequently said that he wanted actors and stage action to consist of "animated hieroglyphs." Artaud's interest in the oriental theater, which became an intense preoccupation after 1931, parallels a concern with the ideogram and the pictogram as opposed to the devitalized word-symbols of the post-Egyptian occident.

The oriental perceives essentially rather than concretely, whereas with the westerner the opposite is the case.[11] Yet the essence is achieved through the impact of images and not through conceptualization, and this presents an anomaly. Ezra Pound has expressed this idea well: "The Egyptians finally used abbreviated pictures to represent sounds, but the Chinese still use abbreviated pictures AS pictures, that is to say, Chinese ideogram does not try to be the picture of a sound, or to be a written sign recalling a sound, but it is still the picture of a thing; of a thing in a given position or relation, or of a combination of things. It *means* the thing or the action or situation, or quality germane to the several things that it pictures." [12]

If Chinese is basically pictographic, it has become so stylized as to defy identification save for the initiated. However, the totally pictographic ancient Mexican "writing" is accessible to the eye, and if scholars are frustrated by the lack of phonetic writing, the uninitiated can only rejoice at the clarity of the symbols. If time has to some extent stripped these of their originally intended magical powers, they are nevertheless juxtaposed in relationships which many, such as Jung, would have us believe are autonomous and common to all mankind. We feel closer to the animistic stimulus of the Aztec, for

18

example, when we contemplate his symbols, than we do to the random stimuli that move the modern occidental artist, which he struggles to conceptualize or portray accurately in words.

Although Artaud does not talk or write about Mexican culture until later in his life, it seems certain that he had read widely about it, as well as about Egyptology and alchemy, in the formative years of the late twenties and early thirties.* We may assume that his interest in Mexico was great prior to his visit in 1936, and many of the extraordinary fragmentary notes edited by Serge Berna and published under controversial conditions as *The Life and Death of Satan-Fire, followed by Mexican Texts for a New Myth* (*Vie et mort de Satan le feu, suivi de textes mexicains pour un nouveau mythe*)[13] appear to have been written before Artaud's trip to Mexico. The poet's deep preoccupation with the discovery of an actual culture compatible with his ideas—a culture in which Artaud hoped to find answers to the ontological questions that plagued him and that he was having little success answering in Europe—is seen in the beginning of "Mexico and Civilization" ("Le Mexique et la civilisation"): "Perhaps it is a baroque idea for a European to go to Mexico in search of the living foundations of a culture the notion of which seems to be crumbling away here; but I admit that the idea obsesses me; in Mexico there is to be found, linked to the earth, lost in the outflows of volcanic lava, vibrant in the Indian blood, the magic reality of a culture, and little would be required, no doubt, for its fires to be materially revived."[14]

Artaud's readings about the cosmogonies and theogonies of the Near, Middle, and Far East, of Egypt, and of pre-Columbian Mexico (which may be inferred from his frequent

---

* We must recall that Artaud was silent in mental institutions from 1937 to 1946. When his faculties were revived through the use of electric shock treatments, he resumed the interests which had been interrupted by illness and we again have references to Mexican culture.

references to the Egyptian and Tibetan "Books of the Dead," the *Popol-Vuh*, the *Tao Teh Ching*, his allusions to Mazdaism, alchemy, and the cabala, and his interest in the tarot cards) understandably led him to consider the possibility that the goal of his quest might exist in the wilderness of Mexico in the midst of some tribe which perhaps had not lost its ties with the ancient traditions of its Toltec, Aztec, or Mayan ancestors.

Artaud's Mexican investigations appear to date from shortly after the 1931 experience with the Balinese dance group; to find expression in the second manifesto of "The Theater of Cruelty" ("Le Théâtre de la cruauté"), with its scenario of *The Conquest of Mexico* (*La Conquête du Mexique*) which Artaud intended at that time to present as his first manifestation of a Theater of Cruelty; and to culminate in his Mexican expedition in 1936.

The period of composition of some of the sections of *The Life and Death of the Late Satan*, which Serge Berna wrongly assumed to have been during and after the Mexican trip, is properly indicated by Paule Thévenin as in the early thirties:

Here, roughly, is the inventory of the manuscripts which he (Berna) had with him and which he asked me to decipher:
the few pages of *The Life and Death of the Late Satan* . . . ;
some notes taken by Antonin Artaud concerning Far Eastern and Mexican religion, apparently taken after he had read on the subject;
some personal notes on separate sheets or on the backs of sheets dealing with religion;
"Mexico and Civilization," a manuscript which was published in incomplete form, the end being in a telegraphic style, but which, according to the indication of a note, *letter to Massignon*, had been written before Artaud left for Mexico;

20

two typewritten pages of an unfinished letter dealing with
Mexico;
  some rough drafts of letters;
  all of this written presumably between 1932 and
1935–36.[15]

Danzel describes the non-phonetic nature of the ancient
Mexican writing whose symbols still speak vividly to us today:

It seems to me that the symbolism of the pre-Hispanic
Mexicans very much merits the interest of the cultural psy-
chologist. Scarcely any other people not yet in possession of
phonetic writing has given us such a wealth of symbolic
signs and images. Yes, it is important to stress that the
Mexicans had no phonetic writing: they had no accurate,
literal means of registering the spoken word. Many conceptions which with us have paled to abstraction were to them
still image and symbol. Much that in our culture has grown
dim and conceptual remained for them concrete and visi-
ble.[16]

Artaud was extremely concerned with the exploitation of the
full stage space in which the rhythms, gestures, and objects
would swirl and writhe in action, the play being made up of
motions, hieratic gestures and postures, pauses, shouts, barks,
sonorous effects, lighting effects, and so forth. Obviously the
ancient Mexican symbol cannot communicate sound or actual
movement to us, but it communicates proportion, stance, gesture, and tension, which is almost a form of rhythm. The
principal sensation is one of violence and cruelty and harsh-
ness of gesture frozen at full strength in the stone or in the
paintings.
  The sacrificial scene in the Codex Nuttall represents the
offering of the heart of the victim to the sun in a gesture

analogous to tearing an ear of corn from the stalk; and the eagle and the jaguar fighting represent the simulated battle between the priest and the victim.[17] The difficulties that arise when we resort to conceptualization are seen in Laurette Séjourné's opinion that the same pictogram represents the struggle of burning water's "igneous mass against matter, which constantly threatens to annihilate it." [18]

Regardless of discrepancies in symbolic interpretation, there is an undeniable aesthetic communication in these ornate yet stark figures, and there is a certain vitality and sense of compositional aesthetic revealed by the arrangement of the hieroglyphs, which need not constitute a regular script or narrative sequence in order to stir us. Whatever the implications of the jaguar and the eagle as linguistic hieroglyphs, we are able to pick out from the swirling and floating figures in the codex the compositional relationship in the proximity and similar alignment of these two groups of figures, the animal paralleling the human. Above the stagelike platform, which we take to be the sacrificial altar, groups are disposed in their various individuated preoccupations which are at the same time urgently interrelated.

The steady, implacable, practiced stroke of the knife of the black-faced priest, the pale inertia of the victim who seems almost to offer his breast to the knife: these hieroglyphs are striking in their ability to transmute the space in which they are disposed into a sacramental arena which to our eyes, in our day, still reverberates with colors, glowing light, and revolving rhythms. These effects are themselves, in their own way, magical, and it was this sort of magic that Artaud wished to implement in the framework of the theater, and in search of which he made his Mexican pilgrimage.

That Artaud was intellectually aware of the theatrical implications of the Mexican hierograms is seen in the following

Sacrificial Scene, detail from the Codex Nuttall, late pre-Conquest Mixtec. From a facsimile published by the Peabody Museum, Cambridge, Massachusetts. Courtesy Peabody Museum and University of Pennsylvania Library.

passage from his lecture "The Theater & the Gods" ("Le Théâtre & les Dieux"), delivered in Mexico City on February 29, 1936:

I studied at length the Gods of Mexico in the Codices, and it appeared to me that these Gods were above all Gods in space, and that the Mythology of the Codices contained a science of space with its Gods like holes of shadows ("trous d'ombres") and its shadows where life growls.

That is to say, to get to the point, that these Gods were not born by accident, but that they are in life as in a theater, and that they occupy the four corners of the consciousness of Man in which are tucked sound, gesture, the word, and the breath which spews forth life.[19]

The extent to which Artaud felt he had found in Mexico the land of inspiration for a theater based on "animated hieroglyphs" is clear in the above passage as well as in numerous others in *The Tarahumaras* (*Les Tarahumaras*), and the appeal seems to be twofold: metaphysical and aesthetic; that is, embodying both symbol and meaningful silhouette or Gestalt: "Theater is an art of space and it is by emphasizing the cardinal points of space that it has a chance of touching life itself. It is in the space haunted by the theater that things find their countenances, and under these countenances the sound of life."[20]

In the two quotations given above, Artaud equates the "science of space" with the "Gods like holes of shadows," and he equates the theater with culture. In these two formulas lie the key to his search and the godliness he attached to the art of the theater.

Elsewhere, Artaud notes that "it is useful to have the *obsession of counting*,"[21] and frequently in his Mexican writings he resorts to enumeration. We are reminded of his interest in astrology and the tarot cards, whose meaning was taught to Artaud by Manuel Cano de Castro [22]:

> *Ten* crosses in a circle and *ten* mirrors. *One* pole, with *three* hierophants on it. *Four* communicants (*two* Males and *two* Females). The epileptic dancer, and *myself*, for whom the rite was performed.
>
> At the feet of each hierophant, *one* hole at the bottom of which the Male and the Female of Nature, represented by the hermaphroditic roots of the Peyote (it is known that Peyote bears the figure of a man and a woman's sexes intertwined), sleep in Matter, that is to say in the Concrete.
>
> And the hole, with a basin of wood or of earthenware turned upside-down over it, represents the Globe of the World. On the basin the hierophants scrape the mixing or separation of the two principles, and they scrape them in the Abstract, that is in the Principle or Beginning. While beneath it those two Principles, incarnate, reside in the Matter, that is to say in the Concrete.[23]

We may apply this divine oneness of the hole to the "holes of shadows" with which Artaud compares the gods of the codices.

Theater and culture are both qualities which cannot be written down, but Artaud felt that they had in common certain characteristics which are perhaps most vividly portrayed in primitive rites. The aim of the theater Artaud envisaged may be divined—if not truly defined—in terms of culture, with which Artaud equates it:

> The true culture can only be understood in terms of space, and it is an oriented culture, as the theater is oriented. . . .
> Culture is a movement of the mind which goes from the

void toward forms, and from the forms returns into the void, into the void as into death. To be cultivated is to burn away forms, to burn away forms in order to attain life.[24] It is to learn to remain erect in the never-ending movement of forms that one destroys one after the other.[25]

Had Artaud been content to try to transpose the Gestalt and the technique of Mexican monuments and codices to Europe, his trip would no doubt have been entirely rewarding. It was Artaud's tragedy, however, that the spiritual sublimation which he had hoped to achieve personally, the key to "l'ÊTRE" or Being, which he had hoped to be given by the distant tribe of the Tarahumaras, failed to materialize, and the Mexican trip was a combination of important discoveries and yet another personal "échec" or setback.

Artaud returned to France dejected and on the brink of total breakdown. The series of setbacks—from the rejection of his poems by the *Nouvelle Revue Française* in the early twenties to the failure of *The Cenci (Les Cenci)* and the Mexican trip—no doubt helped convince him that he had been hexed ("envoûté") during his trip up a Mexican mountain. The conviction that he was under a spell remained with Artaud for the rest of his life.[26]

If the Mexican trip had a deleterious effect on Artaud's mental stability, it did at least confirm many of his ideas about the primitive theater. If Artaud did not find exactly what he expected, it is no doubt because what he sought was unattainable anywhere. But that he found in part what he was seeking is evident from his accounts of the culture he encountered among the Tarahumara Indians.

The two rites Artaud enthusiastically describes in his Mexican writings are those he calls the Tutuguri, or sun rite, and the Ciguri, or all-night peyote ceremony. The rituals are dramatic and Artaud describes them vividly.[27]

25

And that's when the old Mexican chief struck me in order to open up once again my conscience, for I was not born to understand the Sun; and then again it is in the hierarchical nature of things that after having passed through the EN-TIRETY, that is to say the multiple, which is things, one returns to the primacy of one, which is Tutuguri or the Sun, only to be dissolved and resuscitated by means of that mysterious operation of reassimilation as comprised in the Ciguri, like a Myth of re-enactment, then extermination, and finally of resolution in the sieve of the extreme expro-priation, just as their priests continue to cry out and affirm in their night-long Dance. For it lasts all night from sun-down to sunrise, but it takes the whole night and collects it as one takes juice from a fruit right down to the life source.[28]

The "rite of the black sun" of the Tarahumaras is described by Artaud in a section of *To Have Done with the Judgment of God* (*Pour en finir avec le jugement de Dieu*). The telegraphic style is characteristic of Artaud's poems, but the imagery of this text makes it scenic and is in some respects more theatri-cal and more "réalisable" than his actual scenarios. Several fragments will convey the action and the spirit of "Tutuguri: The Rite of the Black Sun" ("Tutuguri: le rite du soleil noir"):

The rite calls for the new sun to pass through
     seven points
before exploding at the orifice of the earth.

And there are six men,
one for each sun
and a seventh man
who is the pure raw sun
cloaked in black and in red flesh.

26

Now, this seventh man
is a horse,
a horse with a man leading it.

.    .    .    .    .    .    .    .    .    .    .

Upon the tearing sound of a drum and a long trumpet
     blast,
most strange,
the six men
who had been laid out,
*rolled* out along the ground,

rise up one after the other like sunflowers
not suns
but spinning earths,*
water lotuses,
and as each rises
an ever more gloomy and *introverted* bong of the drum
     sounds
until suddenly there arrives, at full gallop,
with dizzying speed,
the last sun,
     the first man,
     the black horse with a
          naked, stark
     naked, and
          virgin man
               on its back.

.    .    .    .    .    .    .    .    .    .

Having finished turning around
they uproot
the crosses from the ground

* ". . . comme des tournesols / non pas soleils / mais sols tournants."
The pun is lost in English.

and the naked man
on the horse
holds aloft
an immense horseshoe
soaked in a cut of his blood.[29]

Perhaps even more ritualistic is the ceremony surrounding
the consumption of peyote, the hallucinogenic agent derived
from cactus buttons and from which mescaline is extracted.
The Mexican Indian, and later the American Indian (who
adopted the custom from his brothers south of the border),
attributed divine powers to this hallucinogenic and used it as
part of a rite of purification.

Artaud's writings from the Mexican period are full of physi-
ological explanations of the mystical realm, and thus are tied
in with his insistence that his spell was physical; and these
explanations reveal how dangerously close Artaud is to his
breakdown. The metaphysical quest, which characterizes Artaud's theories of the earlier part of the decade—expressed in
*The Theater and Its Double* (*Le Théâtre et son double*),
predominates over physical explanations such as the supersen-
sory knowledge of the arrival of the plague on the part of the
Sardinian viceroy in "The Theater and the Plague" ("Le
Théâtre et la peste"). In the Mexican writings we encounter
more and more physical explanations for metaphysical phe-
nomena. This does not make the explanations more readily
accessible to the intellect. On the contrary, it removes them
from rational acceptance. In such passages as that of "The
Peyote Rite" ("Le Rite du Peyotl"), in which Artaud desig-
nates the liver as the filter of the unconscious, his "separation"
is total, his theories are reduced to the level of the most
maligned practices of the alchemists and the discarded theories of medieval medicine:

28

It is in the human liver that one finds the secret alchemy and the labor by way of which the self or ego of each individual chooses what best suits it, adapts it or rejects it from among the many sensations, emotions, and desires which the unconscious provides him with and which make up his appetites, his conceptions, his true beliefs, and his *ideas*. It is at this point that the "I" becomes conscious and that its power of appreciation, of extreme organic discrimination, becomes evident. Because that is when *Ciguri* works to separate what exists from what does not exist. The liver seems, then, to be the organic filter of the *Unconscious*.[30]

However, from the standpoint of dramatic gesture, the peyote dance and ritual contain elements germane to Artaud's concepts. It is significant that the various gestures of the priests and participants are described in terms of letters and are reminiscent of Artaud's animated hieroglyphs; and it is also significant that Artaud hoped to discover some type of stenography with which he could transcribe his "language" of the theater:

The priest touched first his spleen and then his liver with his right hand while with the left he struck the earth with a staff. Each of these touches was echoed by a distant attitude of the man and the woman, at one moment, of desperate, haughty affirmation, at the next moment, of enraged renunciation. But after several hurried blows struck by the priest, who now held his cane with both hands, they advanced rhythmically toward one another, their elbows held wide and their hands joined in two animate triangles. And at the same time their feet sketched circles on the earth and something resembling the parts of letters, an S, a U, a J, a V.[31]

The dance between the man and the woman continues through eight gestures, and on the eighth gesture the hierophant places himself to the north for the climax of the rite, and he assumes a height and terrible splendor like those of the *shite* on buskins in the Noh:

> Upon the eighth gesture they looked toward the Priest who then assumed a dominating and menacing air at the extreme end of the Holy of Holies, where things are in contact with the North. And with his staff he traced a large 8 in the air. But the cry he uttered at that moment had what it takes to revolutionize the *labor of death throes of the dead man black with his ancient sin,* as it is stated in the old buried poem of the Mayas of Yucatan. . . . This cry of the Priest was as though made to reinforce the outline traced in the air. While crying out in this manner the Priest made a sudden movement and represented in the air with his whole body and on the earth with his feet the same figure of eight, until he closed this eight on the South side.[32]

According to Artaud, the Tarahumara Indians live in a veritable communion with the divine Male-Female archetype, surrounded by "signs" in their man-made habitat and in nature, and, if they are primitive from the scientific point of view, they are extremely sophisticated in their awareness of divinity, and they are obsessed by philosophy, fearing most of all the loss of consciousness. According to Artaud, they are aware not only of the duality of the universe,[33] but also of the tension and vitality inherent in the balance of opposites:

> Now, if the people of the Tarahumara tribe wear a headband, sometimes a white one, sometimes a red one, it is not to affirm the duality of the two opposing forces, it is to indicate that *inside* the Tarahumara race the Male and the

30

Female in Nature exist simultaneously and that the Tarahumaras benefit from their combined forces. They wear, so to speak, their philosophy on their heads, and that philosophy combines the action of the two opposing forces in a semi-divine equilibrium.[34]

The peyote dance in many respects resembles the Tutuguri rite:

During the day, two kids had been killed. And now I beheld, on a throne made of a stripped tree which was cut in the form of a cross as well, the lungs and the hearts of the animals trembling in the night wind.[35]

On the side where the sun rises they erected ten crosses of irregular height but symmetrically arrayed; and to each cross they attached a mirror.[36]

This area, which Artaud calls a "hearth" ("foyer"), is drenched in magical powers, and around it lies a zone where no Indian dares to venture, for "it is told that, in this circle, stray birds fall down and pregnant women feel their embryos disintegrate."[37] The priests spend the night going through their motions and "establishing the lost connections, with triangular gestures which slice in strange ways the perspectives of the air."[38]

There is no doubt that Antonin Artaud felt it his calling to try to communicate to the world the secrets which he, as an initiate, held. There is a desperate urgency about the Mexican writings, as though he sensed that if he could not convince people of his truths now, for once truly bear witness ("prendre date"), he would never be able to; and he tried to signal to the world his message as he went under—one of the "tortured souls who are burned at the stake and who make signs from their pyres."[39]

31

The ancient Mexican rites of human sacrifice, and other rites in which it was simulated, cannot be surpassed for cruelty. If one single incident in the occidental tradition is their equal, it is the moment in Greek mythology when Atreus cuts up and serves to his brother Thyestes at a banquet Thyestes' own children. That story was immortalized dramatically by Seneca in his tragedy, *Thyestes*.

Among the Greek and Roman dramatists, Seneca appealed to Artaud the most. In a letter to Jean Paulhan dated December 16, 1932, Artaud wrote:

I am in the midst of reading Seneca—and it seems crazy to me that people have been able to mix him up with the moralist tutor of God knows what emperor of the decline—or at least the Tutor was this one but older and made desperate through magic. Whatever the case may be, this one I have been reading is, as far as I am concerned, the greatest tragic author in history, an initiate of the Secrets and one who was even better than Aeschylus at putting them into words. I weep upon reading his inspired drama, and in it behind the word I sense syllables crepitating in the most ghastly manner with the transparent boiling up of the forces of chaos. And this gives me a thought: once cured, I intend to organize dramatic readings—for a man who denounces the idea of a text in the theater, that's not a bad one—public readings in which I will read Tragedies by Seneca, and all the subscribers we can find for the Théâtre de la Cruauté will be invited. One cannot find anywhere a better *written* example of what is meant by cruelty in the theater than in all the Tragedies of Seneca, and especially in *Thyestes*.[40]

We cannot be certain how many of Seneca's tragedies Artaud read, only that he was very familiar with *Thyestes*, having, shortly after writing the above letter, done an adaptation of that play which is unfortunately now lost. Very little is known about Artaud's adaptation. In a postscript to Jean-Louis Barrault which, according to the latter, was written around 1935, Artaud appears to have substantially completed his play: "And I must also read to you my tragedy: *The Torture of Tantalus (Le Supplice de Tantale)*." [41]

In a draft of what was no doubt to be a press release concerning his play, Artaud describes *The Torture of Tantalus* as one of the "Great Myths of the Past" which dissimulate pure forces.[42] Artaud reiterates his concept of exorcism through catastrophe which makes the viewer vulnerable to those pure forces:

Whereas most people remain impervious to a subtle discourse whose intellectual development escapes them, they cannot resist effects of physical surprise, the dynamism of cries and violent movements, visual explosions, the aggregate of tetanizing ("tétanisants") effects called up on cue and used to act in a direct manner on the physical sensitivity of the spectator.

Carried along by the paroxysm of a violent physical action which no sensitivity can resist, the spectator finds his over-all nervous system becoming sharpened and refined, he becomes more apt to receive the wave length of rarer emotions and of the sublime ideas of the Great Myths which through the particular performance will attempt to reach him with their physical conflagration-like force.[43]

It is clear that Artaud feels a collective effect, not unlike the nervous disintegration leading to catharsis in "The Theater and the Plague," may be obtained in the theatrical event. It is interesting that his desire to reach large numbers of spectators was reflected in the projected setting which was to be extratheatrical, "a factory or exhibition hall."

Although *The Torture of Tantalus,* or *Atreus and Thyestes,* as Artaud has also called this play, is lost, there is some hope that it will one day be found, as the manuscripts of Antonin Artaud were widely dispersed during his last years and in the hours immediately following his death. We can examine Seneca's play, however, as an antecedent and perhaps even conjecture as to the nature of Artaud's adaptation.

Aristotle advised that "the best tragedies are founded on the story of a few houses—on the fortunes of Alcmaeon, Oedipus, Orestes, Meleager, Thyestes, Telephus, and those others who have done or suffered something terrible."[44] He elsewhere writes that "when the tragic incident occurs between those who are near or dear to one another—if, for example, a brother kills, or intends to kill, a brother, a son his father, a mother her son, a son his mother, or any other deed of the kind is done— these are the situations to be looked for by the poet."[45]

Of all the houses in classical mythology, the house of Atreus is perhaps richest in malediction and foul deeds of the sort prescribed by Aristotle, and, indeed, from the initial curse upon Tantalus to the absolution of Orestes, almost all the characters have both done and suffered terrible things, and it is but natural that many tragedies should have been written about that house. Seneca's tragedy is based upon the incident in the legend when Atreus, having lured his brother Thyestes back to his kingdom, feeds the unsuspecting Thyestes the bodies of the latter's sons.[46]

It is not difficult to see why this play fascinated Artaud sufficiently to take its place in the plans for the Théâtre de la Cruauté alongside *The Cenci* and *The Conquest of Mexico.* The play has a basic violence of catastrophic proportion, embracing a whole household throughout generations, a violence which recurs in various forms in the individual households of the members of the lineage of Tantalus. Artaud writes of the forces at play in the great myth: "These monsters are evil as only blind forces can be, and there is no theater, I feel, save on a level which has not yet become human." [47]

Artaud appears to have found elements in *Thyestes* that may be related to the ideas in *The Theater and Its Double,* for there are some fragmentary notes pertaining to the lost adaptation that are reminiscent of various sections of *The Theater and Its Double,* and particularly "The Theater and the Plague":

> The Fury of heaven,
> see Ecclesiastes,
> see Book of Job.
> Tantalus: Man.
> The Burdens of Heredity.
> No Free Will.
> Classification of Evil.
> To Understand One's Fate.
> Man, plaything of god, Plaything of himself.
> Reckon with the powers.
> Heroism: to accept epidemic.[48]

Artaud no doubt liked the irreversible, relentless rhythm imposed from without by the curse of generations—a curse which we understand will go on grinding away at the foundations of this house forever, if need be, in order to wear down the ever more inured sinners.

It is true that Seneca's play is full of rhetoric, something Artaud sought to eliminate from the theater, but at the same time there is great conciseness, of thought (as in the dialogue on monarchical *noblesse oblige*), and of imagery (as in the messenger's description of the slaughter of Thyestes' sons). In fact, the two elements combine in this particular play to give us a mise en scène or scenario for a play representative of the Theater of Cruelty. This is so because the messenger's wordy description is itself eminently stageable and in an Artaudian vein. Thus, it may well have been Artaud's intention to stage such passages as the slaughter of the boys and perhaps Tantalus' description of his punishment. That some such transposition from text to stage image was likely is intimated by Artaud in his prospectus for the play: "All the Great Myths of the Past dissimulate pure forces. They were only invented to make those forces durable and manifest. And outside their scholarly and literary casing, Antonin Artaud wants to attempt, by means of an adaptation of a Mythic tragedy, to express their natural forces on the stage and thus to deliver the theater to its true goal and calling." [49]

The Senecan passage in which the messenger describes the murder of Thyestes' sons and their culinary preparation is amazingly like a scenario. The mysterious and desolate area, where one expects Mithraic sacrifices might take place, is the stage, and this *décor* is pierced by sounds of noisy trumpets and screeching axles, and

> Under the shade stands a dismal spring, whose sluggish water sticks in the black marsh; such is the ugly pool of ominous Styx by which the gods swear. It is rumored that in the blind of night the gods of the dead groan from this place, clanking chains sound in the grove and ghosts howl. . . . More, the whole forest flickers with tongues of flames and the high balks glow without fire. Repeatedly the grove reverberates with threefold barking, repeatedly the palace is shaken with huge phantoms.[50]

Thus we have the stage set by the messenger, whose tale is a complete play within the play, with melancholy colors and with a dead light shattered by flame-licks and pallid glimmerings, the whole echoing with bellows, cries, trumpets, and barkings, in the Artaudian manner.

36

Seneca's description of the inner garden must have been received with great sympathy by Artaud, for barely a year before discovering Seneca, he had delivered his lecture on "Metaphysics and the Mise en Scène" ("La Mise en scène et la métaphysique") [51] which contained a description of Lucas van Leyden's painting of *Lot and His Daughters* in which Artaud's description of the painting greatly resembles Seneca's passage. Let us cite several paragraphs from Artaud's text:

> To the left of the painting and toward the back, a black tower rises to a prodigious height, shored up at its base by a whole system of boulders, plants, zigzag roads marked with milestones, dotted here and there with houses. And with a fortunate perspective effect, one of the roads breaks off at a given point from the hodgepodge through which it has been picking its way, crosses a bridge, to fall finally under the rays of that stormy light which overflows from between the clouds and which randomly sprinkles the countryside.[52]

> Furthermore there is, in Lot and his daughters, an idea of sexuality and reproduction, with Lot seemingly put there to profit abusively of his daughters, like a hornet.[53]

> And it happens that in the crackling of fireworks, through the nocturnal bombardment of stars, rockets, and solar bombs, we suddenly see before our very eyes in a hallucinatory light, protruding in relief against the night, certain details of the countryside: trees, the tower, mountains, houses, whose illumination and apparition will remain definitively linked in our mind to the idea of that sonorous tearing sound.[54]

In Greek and Roman tragedy, violence was for the most part relegated to the wings. Elizabethan tragedy did not actually commit the foulest crimes on the stage but did bring violence before the audience by performing battles, duels, and other brutal scenes in full view. In fact, one of the richest lodes of solar drama is the Elizabethan revenge tragedy, and it is not surprising that Artaud should have turned to that drama in projecting his plans for a Theater of Cruelty. Three plays Artaud admired were John Webster's *The Duchess of Malfi* and *The White Devil* and Cyril Tourneur's *The Revenger's Tragedy*, which was specifically intended for production by the Théâtre Alfred Jarry, apparently in the 1927–28 season, since it is referred to as a future production in Artaud's 1926–27 prospectus.[55] In the later manifesto for the Théâtre Alfred Jarry's 1928 season, Artaud wrote of this play in relation to Vitrac's *Victor* which was to precede it in the schedule he envisaged at that moment:

> Second on the list, *The Revenger's Tragedy* by Cyril Tourneur. We are not philosophers or reconstructors. We are men who are striving to vibrate and to cause to vibrate, to vibrate in unison. If we no longer believe in a theater of amusement, derivation, filth, and fatuousness, we do believe in that sort of exhaustion on an elevated plane upon which the theater guides life as well as thought. We think that after a crucible play like *Victor*, in which an entire period is melted down and remolded, a big, noisy, grandiose, exalting opus like *The Revenger's Tragedy*, which is furthermore a time-tested masterpiece, will correspond to our way of feeling, to our way of thinking. We shall, therefore, put it on." [56]

Artaud was never to produce *The Revenger's Tragedy*, however.

The revenge tragedy that most fascinated him—which he was never to produce either—was John Ford's *'Tis Pity She's a Whore*. After his description of the devastating effects of the plague in "The Theater and the Plague," Artaud relates them to the theatrical event. The unbridled actions of the person who had been encrusted with "civilization" but is now stripped bare are enacted amid the carnage and violence of the pestiferous city, acted out, as it were, in a "triumph of black forces," [57] unraveled in a desolate landscape under a strange sun. The dark forces behind the plague are shared by the theater which, like the plague, is a collective experience: "It, like the plague, contains some sort of strange sun, a light of abnormal intensity in which the difficult and even the impossible itself suddenly become our natural element. And *'Tis Pity She's a Whore* by Ford, like all truly valid theater, is bathed in the dazzling light shed by that strange sun." [58]

If Artaud was enthusiastic about Seneca in 1932, he was no less enthusiastic about Ford's play in "The Theater and the Plague," which was delivered as a lecture at the Sorbonne on April 6, 1933.[59] The defiance of the two principals, Giovanni and Annabella, and the scope of their unrepenting rebellion are similar to the same attributes in Atreus in *Thyestes*, and the implacable march from evil to greater evil is, if possible, more terrifying, more savagely brutal, than in the Roman play. The siblings' actions, even in their horribleness, have a certain casualness that no doubt appealed to Artaud, for Giovanni and Annabella are described in their own dimension, which at no time indicates that they could conceivably behave otherwise and which therefore allows the difficult and the impossible to become their normal element. Their attitude and the acts which illustrate that attitude burst out of the confines of any readily understandable ethic to create an ethic of their own, predicated on urges diametrically opposed to those endorsed by civilized society. The absolute freedom from moral preconceptions that occurs in a universal catastrophe is approximated by the young couple's immoral and blasphemous behavior (which

Giovanni justifies, however, with arguments as sensible as those that would decree their behavior immoral): "If one is looking for an example of absolute liberty in revolt, Ford's *'Tis Pity She's a Whore* provides a poetic example linked to the image of absolute danger." [60]

*'Tis Pity She's a Whore* could well serve as the handbook of the metaphysical rebel, or of the destructionist, for it is one of the great works in the tradition of the apotheosis of evil, particularly since the characters involved are not demonic stereotypes but superficially normal people.

*'Tis Pity She's a Whore* was first acted "at the Phoenix in Drury Lane by the Queen's Servants, and published in 1638." [61] Despite certain similarities with the typical Elizabethan play—the inevitable sword fights, the corpse-strewn stage in Act V, subplots, and cases of disguise, eavesdropping, and mistaken identity—the over-all tone is quite different. Whereas *Hamlet* is psychological in essence, in that the play is as concerned with the purgation of the protagonist as with audience catharsis, *'Tis Pity She's a Whore* evolves on the level of action, and the action is neither condemned nor praised, but since it is presented candidly and without moral reservation or psychological hesitation on the part of character or author, we may say that the play is an implicit apologia for the action presented, or at least as presented theatrically. Here, in brief, is that action.

The scene is Parma. Florio has a son, Giovanni, and a daughter, Annabella. Annabella is the subject of the attention of several suitors, the noble Soranzo, the nefarious Grimaldi, and the silly Bergetto. The play does not waste a moment in getting to the point of conflict. In the opening confessional scene, Giovanni not only confesses to the friar that he is in love with his sister but even attempts to rationalize such a relationship. Giovanni then consummates his love for his sister, with the knowledge of her tutoress, Putana. Subsequently, they pursue their relationship and Annabella thwarts any attempts on the part of her father to wed her to Bergetto or Soranzo, until she becomes pregnant and is persuaded by the friar to marry Soranzo.

When Soranzo becomes aware of Annabella's pregnancy, in a cruel and stirring scene he threatens to kill her if she does not tell him the name of the father of her unborn child. She steadfastly refuses to divulge Giovanni's name, but from the weaker Putana, Soranzo's servant Vasques is able to coax the truth, after which he puts out her eyes.

Soranzo swears revenge and holds his customary birthday party, to which he invites all the principals of the drama. It is his intention to allow Giovanni into a room where he has locked Annabella, and, when they have succumbed to their passion and start to make love, to disclose their act and kill them. However, Annabella and Giovanni realize that they have been discovered, and Giovanni, while embracing his sister, stabs her to death, thus thwarting Soranzo.

In the final scene, Giovanni enters the banquet hall with a heart upon his dagger. The guests understandably fail to realize what Giovanni is holding aloft, and even after he has proclaimed that it is the heart of Annabella, the truth is only understood when confirmed by Vasques who has gone into the bedroom to investigate. In a general debacle, Florio dies of a heart attack, Soranzo draws his sword and is killed by Giovanni, who is then killed by Vasques and the *banditti* hired for the assassination of the lovers.

This fantastic play is one of action—even the soliloquies are not psychological but germane to the narrative—and the action is amazing. Here we have no conflict over the moral dilemma of "Should we or shouldn't we?" which has permeated occidental tragedy since the Greeks, but rather an ever-crescendoing affirmation of the commitment of the young lovers. And the crescendo goes on and on to demonic heights one would think unattainable without passing out of the range of human perception and comprehension. The moment when Giovanni enters in the last scene and we hesitate to grasp the full force of his act, we are confronted for an instant with an animated hieroglyph whose secrets horrify us when we learn them; and we discover them before the other characters in the play, as we have been, from our vantage point as spectators, witnesses to the sacrifice. The dramatic paroxysm of the immolation of Annabella would seem total, final; but there is beyond that the implosion of Giovanni's "finest hour," in which he not only seizes the initiative from his enemies but is able to watch them—as Atreus watched Thyestes—not *being* miserable, but *becoming* miserable as the truth of his horrible act dawns on them. The fact that Giovanni has forestalled their revenge lends an extramoral nobility to his gesture of holding aloft the heart, the waving of the banner of evil, the triumph of black forces. As Artaud writes of that moment, "when we think that we have arrived at the paroxysm of horror, blood, outraged laws, namely poetry consecrated by revolt, we are forced to go still further in a dizzying impulse that nothing can stop." [62]

Artaud's only full-length play was *The Cenci* which he put on in his Théâtre de la Cruauté in 1935. *The Cenci* was, as Artaud states in a subtitle, adapted from Stendhal and Shelley. Like *'Tis Pity She's a Whore*, the Cenci story takes place in Renaissance Italy and deals with incest. This, however, is a true story from the State Archives in Rome which relates the history of a noble family, that of Count Cenci, who was purported to have raped his daughter Beatrice and in turn been murdered by her.

The story was a popular source of various literary adaptations, such as the tragedy in five acts, *Béatrix Cenci,* by Astolphe de Custine, which was produced in 1833; the 1825 brochure published by Vernal et Tenon in Paris entitled *The*

*Story of the Cenci Family: A Work Translated from the Italian Original Discovered in the Vatican Library by the Abbé Angelo Maio, Curator of the Library (Histoire de la famille Cenci*, etc.), which has been attributed to Stendhal; [63] the *Tale of the Death of Giacomo and Beatrice Cenci and Lucretia Petroni (Relation de la mort de Giacomo et Béatrix Cenci et de Lucrèce Petroni)* published in the second volume of the "miscellany" of the Société des Bibliophiles and attributed by some to Stendhal; [64] and Niccolini's *Beatrice Cenci*, inspired by Shelley.[65] But by far the most important adaptations are the prose account, "The Cenci" ("Les Cenci"), by Stendhal, and Shelley's tragedy, *The Cenci*, both of which were sources for Artaud's version.

"The Cenci" by Stendhal appeared anonymously in the *Revue des Deux-Mondes* on July 1, 1837, and was reprinted in *L'Abesse de Castro* (Dumont, 1839). It later became part of the *Italian Chronicles (Chroniques italiennes)* edited by R. Colomb in the Michel Levy edition of Stendhal's *Complete Works* which appeared in 1855.[66]

Stendhal's opening pages contain a discussion of Don Juanism as a malady of modern man: "Don Juan would have been an effect without a cause in antiquity. . . . Only the government spoke of abstention; it forbade things which could harm the fatherland." [67] Don Juanism is mercurial, rebellious, transitory. As Camus points out, "the Byronic hero, incapable of love, or capable only of an impossible love, suffers from spleen. He is alone, languid; his condition exhausts him. If he is to feel alive, it must be in the terrible exaltation of a brief and ferocious action." [68] The Don Juan figure suffers the languid sexuality of potential destructive bestiality, and we are reminded once more of Artaud's description of Lot in van Leyden's painting, in which the patriarch is portrayed in an attitude of latent sexual violence. Don Juan is, for Stendhal, a

43

strictly modern occidental hero [69] in search of self-gratification and oblivion, be it only the momentary oblivion of physical love.

Stendhal considers that Cenci embodies the archetypal Don Juan: "It is in Italy and only in the sixteenth century that this peculiar character appeared for the first time." [70] Given that Don Juanism would be pointless or impossible in the days of the ancients and that its actions could only constitute Don Juanism when they came to be proscribed by what Stendhal called the "ascetic institutions" which arose in the early sixteenth century, Don Juanism, as such, was, indeed, first found in the period of Count and Beatrice Cenci.

Stendhal had bought permission to copy a contemporary account of the Cenci murder and execution and was particularly pleased that the account he presents in almost literal translation is in Roman Italian and written on September 14, 1599, several days after the execution of Beatrice.[71] Here, as reported by Stendhal, are the essentials of the story of Count Cenci—born in Rome in 1527 and murdered in 1598—whose "role as an unadulterated Don Juan . . . is here exposed in all its horror." [72]

Count Francesco Cenci was a very rich man, having been left a great fortune by his father, Monsignor Cenci, who had amassed the wealth while treasurer for Pope Pius V. Francesco enjoyed a generally good reputation until people began to whisper about his peculiar love affairs, "brought to a successful culmination by even more peculiar means," [73] in which he sought ever greater novelty and for which he was repeatedly required to purchase absolution from the Church: witness the cryptic entry in his accounts of an expense of three thousand five hundred piastres "for the adventures and *peripezie* of Toscanella . . . *e non fu caro* ('and it was not too much to pay')." [74]

Cenci married a rich woman by whom he had seven children, after which she died. He shortly thereafter married Lucretia Petroni, who remained childless. Even by the moral standards of sixteenth-century Rome Cenci's character left a great deal to be desired: "The least vice to be held against Francesco Cenci was a propensity for an infamous love; the greatest was not to believe in God. In his lifetime he was never seen entering a church." [75] Thrice imprisoned for his "infamous loves," Cenci was required to pay dearly for his freedom. What passed for his only good deed was the construction of a church to St. Thomas in the courtyard of his huge palace—and this he did only that he might have before his eyes at all times the tombs of his children, whom he hated with a vengeance.

On the occasion of Cenci's third imprisonment, three of his sons, Giacomo, Rocco, and Cristoforo, begged Pope Clement VIII to execute their father for all the dishonor he had brought to their house, but their request was refused. Released from prison, Cenci took out his fury on his two daughters, who lived with him in the Cenci palace, beating them mercilessly. The elder daughter escaped by petitioning the pope to marry her off, and the younger, Beatrice, bore the brunt of his anger. In order that she not escape in the same way, Cenci sequestered her in the palace at the age of fourteen and even brought her food to her himself.

Sometime during this period Cenci fell in love with his daughter. Rocco and Cristoforo were killed in an altercation, and Cenci said that his dream was to bury the last of his children and set fire to his palace. When Beatrice was sixteen, Cenci "tried, with threats and by force, to rape his own daughter Beatrice who was already by then tall and beautiful; he shamelessly entered her bed, stark naked. He walked about the rooms of his palace with her, he being completely naked; then

45

he led her into his wife's bed, in order that by the gleam of the lamps poor Lucretia might see what he was doing with Beatrice." [76]

A nuance of Cenci's evil is seen in the fact that he attempted to seduce Beatrice by telling her that when a father had relations with his daughter, the children born of that union were always saints, that all saints were born in this manner, and that their maternal grandfathers were their fathers.

With the help of a Monsignor Guerra, who was attracted to Beatrice, the sequestered daughter and mother communicated their plan to kill Cenci to the scion Giacomo. Aid was enlisted of Marzio and Olimpio, two of Cenci's vassals whom he had betrayed.

Cenci intended to spend the summer at the Petrella castle, and it was decided that he be killed on his way there to make it appear that brigands had committed the murder, but a misunderstanding permitted him to pass the ambush safely.

At Petrella, Cenci redoubled his abuses of the two women. Beatrice called Marzio and Olimpio under her window and sent letters by them to Guerra. It was agreed that the two vassals would personally undertake the crime for a thousand piastres. It was originally planned that they should kill Cenci on the Day of the Virgin, but Lucretia demurred for religious reasons and finally September 9, 1598, was selected. Cenci was drugged with opium, and Marzio and Olimpio were led to the bedroom where he was sleeping soundly. The vassals dared not commit the murder until Beatrice threatened to do it herself. They returned to the room and drove a spike into the count's eye and another into his throat. Beatrice gave Olimpio a fat purse and Marzio a gold-braided mantle which had belonged to the count and sent them away.

The women withdrew the nails and threw the corpse, wrapped in a sheet, through a window near the jakes, in the hope that it would be thought Cenci had awakened during the night and fallen from the window while on his way to relieve himself.

The crime was discovered. Olimpio had been killed in a fight, but Marzio was taken into custody and confessed all, only to retract his confession and die under torture. The case was about to be dropped when the brigand who had killed Olimpio told the entire story. Guerra disguised himself as a coal vendor, made himself known about Rome, and then passed through the guard at the town gate and disappeared.

Lucretia confessed, and later Beatrice did too. There were appeals to Clement VIII, who reviewed the case. He was on the point of pardoning the two women when he heard of the matricide of the Marquise Constance Santa Croce at the hands of her son Paolo. As a result he rejected the appeal. A younger Cenci brother, Bernard, was pardoned, but he was required to watch as Lucretia and Beatrice were decapitated and Giacomo was bludgeoned to death on September 11, 1599.

Perhaps the most celebrated version of the Roman story is *The Cenci,* by Percy Bysshe Shelley, written in 1819. There are some variations on the actual story as conveyed to us by Stendhal. The principal differences, other than the obvious differences of poetic format, and so forth, are that Monsignor Guerra is replaced by the prelate Orsino, and we have the introduction of Cardinal Camillo, the servant Andrea, and the pope's legate Savella, whose name Shelley no doubt derived from the name of the prison, the Corte Savella, where Lucretia and Beatrice were held. Shelley also prudently replaces Cenci's history of sexual crimes with one of capital crimes, such as murder.

Shelley tries to alleviate the drama-ridden horrors of history by emphasizing the poetic ideal, achieving a suspension or balance bearable for the spectator: "This story of the Cenci is indeed eminently fearful and monstrous: anything like a dry exhibition of it on the stage would be insupportable. The

47

person who would treat such a subject must increase the ideal, and diminish the actual horror of the events, so that the pleasure which arises from the poetry which exists in these tempestuous sufferings and crimes may mitigate the pain of the contemplation of the moral deformity from which they spring." [77]

This metamorphosing of life's horror into imaginative and dramatic art is touched upon by Freud in a paraphrase of Aristotle in "Relation of the Poet to Day-dreaming" of 1908:

> The unreality of this poetical world of imagination, however, has very important consequences for literary technique; for many things which if they happened in real life could produce no pleasure can nevertheless give enjoyment in a play—many emotions which are essentially painful may become a source of enjoyment to the spectators and hearers of a poet's work. [78]

We might venture to conjecture that Artaud would acknowledge the poetry in the crime, but he would reverse the cathartic effect described by Shelley, saying that the contemplation of the moral deformity in man gives rise to the tempestuous poetry of suffering.

Shelley says, in keeping with Artaud's ideas, that

> Imagination is as the immortal God which should assume flesh for the redemption of mortal passion. It is thus that the most remote and the most familiar imagery may alike be fit for dramatic purposes when employed in the illustration of strong feeling, which raises what is low, and levels to the apprehension that which is lofty, casting over all the shadow of its own greatness. [79]

The theater of revolt, or solar drama, as we have defined it and seen it exemplified in these plays and dramatic traditions important in the development of Artaud's dramatic concepts, was not replaced by the theater of stasis, or lunar drama. The latter existed alongside the former, but, whereas solar drama enjoyed pre-eminence through the nineteenth century, static or lunar drama tended to take over the limelight as messianic drama declined during the symbolist period, the interwar years of the dadaist and surrealist movements, and especially after World War II, with the advent of what has come to be called the Theater of the Absurd.

# Lunar Drama and Artaud

Antonin Artaud tended to prefer solar drama to lunar drama. This was particularly true of the later years of his life. However, we are confronted with an anomaly in that Artaud, while advocating the cruel gesture pushed to the *nth* degree, also admired the stylized restraint and the sense of fatality of such lunar theater as that of the orient, which is generally, despite shouts and monsters, a theater of inevitability and resignation.

If one can isolate any single incident as most important in the formation of Artaud's dramatic ideas, it is without doubt the Balinese dance performance at the Colonial Exposition in Paris in 1931. Paul Arnold writes that "in 1931, at the Colonial Exposition, Artaud attended a performance of the Balinese Theater which molded his dramatic doctrine. From that day forth he began to outline his Theater of Cruelty in a series of essays collected in 1938 under the title *The Theater and Its Double*." [80]

Evidence of the influence of oriental theater on Artaud's dramatic theories is omnipresent in his work. The principal essays which pay respects to the oriental tradition are "On the Balinese Theater" ("Sur le théâtre balinais"), "Oriental Theater and Occidental Theater" ("Théâtre oriental et théâtre occidental"), and the first manifesto for "The Theater of Cruelty" ("Le Théâtre de la cruauté"). "An Affective Athleticism" ("Un Athlétisme affectif") and "The Seraphim Theater" ("Le Théâtre de séraphin") are profoundly concerned with the Male-Female duality of the cosmos at the animistic level, particularly as examined by the orientals, cabalists, and alchemists. These essays, with the exception of "The Seraphim Theater," were collected in *The Theater and Its Double;* "The Seraphim Theater" was meant to be included as well but was left out through some unexplained oversight.[81]

We shall examine these essays in detail in another part of this study, but let me mention at this point that the oriental theater not only imparted a certain spirit to the dramatic concepts of Artaud, but actually provided him with certain definite models for the structure of plays as well as the structure of the theater itself. The spirit is reflected in statements like: "I propose a return in the theater to the elementary magical idea, picked up by modern psychoanalysis, which consists of bringing about the cure of a patient by making him assume the external attitude corresponding to the state to which one would seek to restore him." [82] Examples of specific recommendations are the frequent suggestions that one use gigantic two- to ten-meter mannequins on stage and Artaud's blueprint for the physical plant of the theater, which coincides almost identically with that of some oriental theaters.

Artaud wrote, for example, in his first manifesto for a Theater of Cruelty that plays should be presented in a large bare hangar or barn, the action going on around the spectators in the four corners of the building with the scenes being played out against whitewashed walls. In addition, "high galleries will run along the entire hall, as in certain pictures by Primitives.[83] These galleries will permit the actors, each time the action so requires, to move from one point to another in the hall, and the action to unfold on all levels and in all directions of perspective, both in height and in depth." [84] This description brings to mind the scaffolding in the Kabuki theater and even in the modern Japanese theater.

The present form of the Japanese stage became fixed probably in the early eighteenth century. It consists of a wide platform at the end of a rectangular hall. A wooden canopy, closely resembling the "heavens" which sheltered the Elizabethan stage against rain, stretches over the central portion of the Japanese acting platform, and is supported on ornamental columns. Doors from the stage give access to the green-room in the back, as in the Elizabethan and Greek stages. Around all the sides of the hall there runs a narrow shelf of stage, known as the *hana-michi,* or flower path. The flower path is joined to the main stage at either end, so that the stage action may be carried on around the whole auditorium.[85]

Artaud's interest in the oriental theater dates back to 1922—and possibly to 1921—when he first knew Dullin. In 1930, before he saw the Balinese dance group, it was already an acknowledged influence: "The Théâtre Alfred Jarry refuses to list all the fragmentary influences it might have been subjected to (such as: Elizabethan theater, Chekhov, Strindberg, Feydeau, etc.) and only will mention . . . the indisputable examples furnished by the *Chinese, Negro-American, and Soviet theaters.*" [86]

Artaud's attraction to the oriental theater is usually dated from his attendance at the Cambodian dances in front of the reconstruction of the temple of Angkor in Marseilles in 1922, the attraction then being precipitated into concepts following the 1931 Balinese experience. However, it would appear that Artaud had already brought to Dullin's Théâtre de l'Atelier in late 1921 the germ of a style and concepts which were akin to the oriental, and Dullin's own great interest in the oriental theater no doubt underscored Artaud's enthusiasm and prepared him for the 1922 Cambodian experience. Dullin wrote a letter to the journal *K, Revue de la Poésie* on the occasion of its homage to Artaud in 1948 recalling Artaud's early days before and immediately after the founding of Dullin's Théâtre de l'Atelier:

> he was diligent and docile in his work . . . except when it came to the practical exercises of diction which he emphatically refused to pursue.[87] He loved our work on improvisation and brought to it a veritable poet's imagination. As I was attracted to the techniques of the oriental theater, he went even much further in that direction than I, and from the practical viewpoint this sometimes became dangerous, as when, for example, in Pirandello's *The Pleasures of Honesty*, in which he played a businessman, he arrived on stage with make-up inspired by the small masks used as models by Chinese actors; a symbolic make-up which was slightly out of place in a modern comedy. Similarly, in *Huon de Bordeaux*, when he interpreted the role of the elder Charlemagne and swept the steps of the throne with a ringleted beard which made him look like a rabid poodle and suddenly straightened up in an imposing attitude which impressed everyone. He played in an amazing manner the old king in *Life Is a Dream*, for which he made the *décor* and the costumes. He had a great personal triumph in a play by Jacinto Grau,[88] in which he played a kind of incarnation

of evil named Urdemala. I can still hear him pronouncing that name while snapping a whip.[89]

Perhaps it should be pointed out that Artaud never sought to bring the oriental mystique intact onto the western stage. He realized that if the occidental theater was to be renewed, it had rather to find again its own archetypes upon which it might construct a primal dramatic language. It was necessary to dig deep into one's own tradition, not cut across the surface to purloin the tradition of another culture. A passage by Yeats sums up the attitude of Artaud as well as of others like Brecht, Genet, O'Neill, and Craig, who were also influenced by oriental theater:

> For some weeks now I have been elaborating my play [*At the Hawk's Well*] in London where alone I can find the help I need, Mr. Dulac's mastery of design and Mr. Ito's genius of movement; yet it pleases me to think that I am working for my own country. Perhaps some day a play in the form I am adapting for European purposes may excite once more, whether in Gaelic or in English, under the slopes of Slieve-na-mon or Croagh Patrick, ancient memories.[90]

In the occidental tradition, with the destruction of God and the extraterrestrial hope he provided, man's philosophical quest turned, of necessity, inward. This centripetency is characteristic of the philosophical climate of the twentieth century and much of the nineteenth century.

If Nietzsche was the principal intellectual and spiritual source for the atheistic writers who followed, he was not the first to proclaim God dead. Of those who foreshadowed Nietzsche, it was Georg Büchner (1813–37) who most interested Artaud. Just as Strindberg's work was to evolve from a

53

messianic theater (*A Dream Play*) to an existential theater (*The Ghost Sonata*), so Büchner's evolved from *Danton's Death*, with its assault on the gods, to the nihilistic, existential *Woyzeck*.[91]

In *Danton's Death*, Büchner's character Tom Payne pronounces the atheist's catechism for the faltering Chaumette:

> Come then, my philosopher Anaxagoras, I must catechise you. There is no God—since either God made the world or He did not. If He did not make it, the world had its germ in itself, and there is no God—since God is only God if He holds in Himself the germ of all being. Now God cannot have made the world, since either creation is eternal like God, or it had a beginning. If it had a beginning, God must have made it at a given point in time. So that God, having rested for eternity, must have become suddenly active— undergone a change in Himself, which made Him apply a new conception—Time. Both of which assumptions are contrary to God's essence. So that God cannot have made the world. Now since we know clearly that a world exists, or at least that we exist, and that, from what I have just said, that world must have had its roots in itself or in some other thing that is not God, there can be no God. *Quod erat demonstrandum.*[92]

The vacancy left by God's dethronement, which in itself is a gesture of revolt and hence what we have called "solar," inspired a drama of negation, desolation, and defeat. This drama of stasis is often grotesque. The grotesque, as a quality, goes back as far as man, but in our time there has been a certain direction in its exploitation. It has become the very stuff of a type of drama whose existence no doubt compelled Lionel Abel to define his genre of metatheater which adopts the fantastic as an essential ingredient.[93] The new concept does

54

not consider the grotesque as comic, but rather as macabre and stirring by virtue of its novelty.

This theater was foreshadowed by Büchner, inaugurated by Jarry, endorsed by Apollinaire, the surrealists, and Artaud, and consolidated by the authors of the so-called Theater of the Absurd. Its relative solar and lunar attributes are at first confusing, but it is essentially lunar for several reasons. This theater of the grotesque is characterized by desolation, defeat, waiting, and self-denigration, and even when the individual episodes—for the theater of the grotesque is frequently made up of brief tableaux—contain actions as violent as murder or suicide, the over-all mood is one of fruitlessness, acquiescence in the futility of life, acceptance of the frailty of the individual, and self-abnegation.*

The theater of the grotesque finds its source not in the messianic act nor in the act for the act's sake but in the drama of crushing defeat, the quality of hopelessness which obsesses the pessimist. Here we are confronted not with Orestes' vengeful murders but rather with his aimless flight from the Furies—or perhaps we have gone beyond that and find in this drama the renouncement of flight from one's fate.

In *Danton's Death*, which is essentially messianic, Danton is defiant of his opponents' condemnation of his majestic behavior. The heroism of his attitude is expressed in the language of cosmic conquest in his dream:

Dreaming? Yes, dreaming. But it wasn't that. Wait, I'll tell you. Oh, my brain's numb. Now I have it. I rode on the world, swung round with her on her axis. She was under me like a wild horse. I straddled her with huge legs—I dug into

---

* Sometimes so episodic are these plays that the sequence of scenes (that is, the play's straight narrative) is impossible to establish by logic. Such is the case with Büchner's unfinished *Woyzeck*, whose various editors have all arrived at different sequences for the episodes.

her mane and held her in. I threw my head back; my hair streamed over gulfs.[94]

But *Danton's Death* contains the germ of the realization of futility in the waking from the dream in terror, in the uselessness of the revolt from the vaster outlook of the universe which shall ride on despite cataclysms which are measurable in human standards only by the number of corpses they create.

In the little fairy tale told by the old woman in *Woyzeck* lie the seeds of the theater of the grotesque:

Once upon a time, there was a poor little child, and no father it had, and no mother it had—all dead. And no one any more in all the world. All dead. So off it went to look for them all night long and all day long. And there was nobody any more in all the world, so it tried to fly up to heaven —and the moon blinked her eyes and looked so kind; but when it came to the moon, the moon was just an old bit of wood. So then it went to the sun; and when it came to the sun, the sun was no more than a dried-up sunflower—and when it came to the stars, the stars were just little golden flies stuck about like a shrike would stick 'em on a sloe—and when it wanted to go back to earth, the earth was just an overturned mug. And it was all alone, and so it sat itself down and cried, and cried, and cried. And there it sits now still—all alone.[95]

This dejected waiting found its ultimate theatrical expression more than a century later in Beckett's *Waiting for Godot* (*En attendant Godot*).

The nihilistic tradition in the theater is primarily expressed in mood, spirit, or quality, rather than action and is a modern dramatic concept in the West; what elevates the great plays of the theater of the grotesque above the merely monstrous is the spirit they convey in their entirety, and that spirit may be

considered lunar and its plays in the static tradition. Therefore, plays which at first appear radically different are essentially compatible. *King Ubu* has not survived because of its
clownish aspects, but for the antiheroic self-humiliation of its
protagonist, who stands in the Grotesque Pantheon beside such
antiheroes as Dostoevski's Underground Man, Büchner's Woyzeck, Brecht's Baal, and Kaiser's Sokrates. In certain plays of
this sort there is no real hero or antihero at all, and the mood
of humiliation itself becomes the protagonist.

Although in the beginning of his theatrical career Artaud
appears to have admired lunar drama of the sort found in the
symbolist plays of Synge and Maeterlinck, his early admiration for Maeterlinck seems to have been gradually replaced by
an admiration for either solar drama or the grotesque category
of lunar drama.

I should like to consider several plays in this latter tradition
which Artaud particularly admired—*Woyzeck, King Ubu,
The Ghost Sonata,* and *Victor;* a cultural movement—
surrealism; and a representative play of the more conventional
type of lunar drama—*Pelléas and Mélisande* (*Pelléas et
Mélisande*).

The plot of *Woyzeck* is very simple, as is the case with most
static or lunar dramas. Woyzeck is a soldier who has had a
child by a girl named Marie. A drum major seduces Marie
away from Woyzeck, who buys a knife and kills the girl.

The real matter of the play is not the murder but the
ludicrous puppet-like behaviour of Woyzeck, who picks up
extra money to supplement his soldier's pay in order to sup-
port Marie by shaving the captain and by being a human
guinea pig for a mad doctor who makes him live solely on peas
to observe his reactions. Woyzeck is not the least bit heroic;
his act of murder is not the least bit defiant, but rather petty
and sordid. His humiliation is complete when he is struck and
knocked down by the drum major.

This play lends itself to quick changes in stage sets, to lighting tricks, and to a variety of human actions. No doubt for Artaud the fascination of the drama lay partly in the implacable and cruel sense of fatality that is woven through it. (We recall that Artaud's pessimism was one of the things that contributed to his expulsion from among the surrealists.) Artaud frequently mentioned his desire to produce *Woyzeck*. He wrote to Louis Jouvet about the play in October, 1931:

> I have a play which I should like to read to you, not in order to reveal its beauties to you which would be silly, but to have you *hear* my interpretation of it, to propose my personal echo of it to you. Nothing these days in the existing theater, already written, seems to me to be more urgently in need of being *performed* than this particular play.[96]

Artaud also took this project to Charles Dullin, hoping to produce *Woyzeck* in the program of reserved Tuesday performances at the Théâtre de l'Atelier—again with no result.[97] It was his intention to have *Woyzeck* as his first production should he succeed in his efforts to create a subsidized theater backed by the *Nouvelle Revue Française:*

> In fact, the *NRF* is not *creating* a theater whose direction has been entrusted to me, but rather has agreed to be a *patron* to the enterprise I am attempting. It has given me its support and the right to use its name.
> The first play I shall produce is Büchner's *Woyzeck*.[98]

Like so many of Artaud's projects this one never materialized.
Artaud saw the dramatic potential of *Woyzeck*'s mood and how it might be sustained through sounds and other effects in a manner akin to the oriental Kabuki theater, in which, as Earle Ernst describes it, "the basic and continuous ground of

the performance is that of unresolved sadness. The constant dwelling on the poignant and the pathetic and the lack of concern for any strong intellectual element are manifested in the Kabuki by the audience's appreciation of prolonged, static scenes whose only dramatic content is long drawn out melancholy." [99] Artaud wrote in the letter to Jouvet mentioned above: "consider only the sorrowfully human sound of this play, the echoes like cries in an underground cavern or in a dream. No man at any period is impervious to the workings of his unconscious, to that which can give blows of a pickax in the fulgurant flint of the unconscious." [100]

Another play which Artaud intended to produce was *King Ubu,* whose author's name was adopted in the title of the Théâtre Alfred Jarry: "The Théâtre Alfred Jarry will put on in the course of the year a production of *King Ubu,* a *King Ubu* adapted to present-day circumstances and played without stylization" [101] Although Artaud elsewhere says that "as for the spirit guiding the Théâtre Alfred Jarry, it draws on the peerless humoristic lesson of *King Ubu,*" [102] it appears that by stripping *King Ubu* of stylization Artaud intended to play up the characteristics which it shared with *Woyzeck* and other nonhumorous plays of the grotesque.

*King Ubu* is not only important in Artaud's dramatic development, it is seminal to twentieth-century grotesque theater. I should like to consider this play, and particularly Jarry's theoretical pronouncements, which are tacitly a manifesto for the theater founded in 1927 by Artaud, Vitrac, and Aron.

The play is an uproarious farce which, minus subplots, deals with the rise to power and fall from power of a boor named Ubu who is urged on by his ambitious wife, Mère Ubu. Ubu turns on his king and kills him, proclaiming himself king of Poland. Ubu becomes a brutal and capricious tyrant, reminiscent of Heliogabalus and Caligula. The enemies of Ubu enlist the aid of the czar of Russia and Ubu is expelled from Warsaw and flees to a cave in Lithuania where he is miraculously reunited with the long lost Mère Ubu. They set sail for their native France which they decide cannot be far off since they are already passing Elsinore!

In this play are found the presentation of the antihero and certain innovations, such as the use of masks, the impersonation of marionettes, and the neglect of customary economies, unities, and illusions traditional to the modern stage. The oriental, classical Greek, and *commedia dell'arte* theaters made use of masks, it is true, and, as Donald Keene points out in his *Japanese Literature,* the oriental theater differs radically from the occidental in that while westerners attempted to make marionettes as lifelike as possible, orientals held puppetry in such high esteem as an art form that in live plays the actors sought to emulate the gestures of marionettes.[103] However, when Jarry wrote *King Ubu* (and for some time after), the mask had been neglected in the occidental tradition since the classical Greek period.

In this case, the use of masked marionette-like actors derived directly from the fact that the play was first conceived as a guignol show and produced as such at the homes of Jarry and his friend Morin.[104] Later, from artists as unlike as O'Neill and Artaud, we have explicit apologias for the use of the mask, but the fact remains that Jarry used them in the 1880's and 1890's.

There are many ancillary points of interest in the history of *King Ubu.* Of particular interest to us are the liminary remarks delivered by Alfred Jarry at the first real commercial production,[105] the articles entitled "On the Uselessness of Drama in the Theater" ("De l'inutilité du théâtre au théâtre")[106] and "Questions of Theater" ("Questions de théâtre"),[107] and the fragments entitled "Twelve Arguments on the Theater" ("Douze Arguments sur le théâtre")[108] which, as Maurice Saillet points out, with the two articles just mentioned,

60

"constitute the theatrical manifesto of the author of *King Ubu*." [109]

From a reading of *King Ubu* and a casual knowledge of the history of its genesis and development as a play, one might feel that Alfred Jarry was, in a sense, a felicitous freak who accidentally created a classic. However, several brief articles and notes by him constitute a miniature organon for a new theater and reflect his deep preoccupation with the idea of theater.

Jarry was concerned, as are most playwrights, with the audience to which the theater should be geared, "whether theater should adapt itself to the masses or the masses adapt themselves to theater." [110] He justly notes that there are essentially two theaters, the popular and "that other theater which is neither a party for its public, nor a lesson, nor an entertainment, but an action." [111] The audience of what he calls the elite, which consists in the whole universe of "five hundred people who might, compared to the infinite mediocrity about us, have a little bit of the Shakespeare and the Leonardo in them," [112] is the audience toward which he slants his apologia for a new and changing theater.

Of greatest interest to us, in connection with subsequent activity on the part of Artaud, are Jarry's more technical arguments concerning the eradication of the old "language" of the stage and the development of a new. The new language Jarry advocated should, he felt, develop its vocabulary in the realms of *décor*, acting, lighting, and sound ("voix").

*Décor*. Jarry denounced categorically the illusionistic-naturalistic *décor*: "There are two sorts of *décor*, interiors and open-air scenes. Both have the pretention of representing real rooms or fields. We will not again consider the question which has been settled once and for all regarding the stupidity of the *trompe-l'œil décor*." [113] He tended to favor the neutral *décor* with few props. He considered a compromise what he

61

called *"heraldic décors,* that is ones which designate in a single uniform color an entire scene or act, with the characters moving harmoniously against the background of that coat of arms." [114] Jarry went even further in his simplification, deeming unpainted canvas or the "reverse side of a scenery flat" adequate—scene changes being indicated by posted signs and props being brought on stage when needed. [115]

*Acting.* "The actor 'makes the face,' and ought to make the whole body, of a character." [116] Jarry lamented the trend toward naturalistic facial acting and desired rather a total personification through body movements; and to this end he advocated the use of the mask as an inhibitor to facial acting as well as for its own intrinsic value. "The actor should substitute for his head, by means of a mask to enclose it, the effigy of the CHARACTER, and that effigy, unlike those of the ancients, will not be characterized by tears or laughter (which are not characters), but will be characterized by the character himself: The Miser, The Hesitant One, The Voracious One amassing his crimes." [117] The basic hieroglyph or ideogram for the actor lies in the mask, the gestures, and the voice, which is to be used as an extension of the mask, conserving a monotonous continuity in keeping with the character. The subtle variations on the underlying theme or character should be achieved not by facial tics but with variegations of the ideogram itself. This is to be done by lighting, the single greatest innovation in the modern occidental theater and one which had not been fully exploited before. As Jarry points out, the ancients played in a light that normally came from the zenith or at such an obtuse angle as to make shadow a negligible element in staging, and the lamentable neglect of the potential dramatic effect of lighting in the traditional theater of the nineties is seen in Jarry's marginal note:

The fashion of the world and the fashion of the theater exert reciprocal influences and not only in modern plays. But it would not be of any use for the public to go to the theater in evening dress; basically the thing is unimportant, but it is irritating to see people ogling one another through their lorgnettes in the theater hall. Doesn't one go to Bayreuth in a traveling suit? And how well all that could be settled by illuminating only the stage! [118]

*Lighting.* In a brilliant passage of "On the Uselessness of Drama in the Theater" Jarry explains in precise terms the function lighting has in varying the archidiom of the character mask which nevertheless subsists "behind these chance variants."

The footlights illuminate the actor according to the hypotenuse of a right-angled triangle in which his body is one of the sides of the right angle. And since the footlights are a series of luminous dots, that is, a line which extends indefinitely, in comparison to the narrowness of the actor's face, to the right and to the left of the point their planes intersect, one must consider the footlights as a single illuminating point placed at an indefinite distance as though it were behind the public.

It follows that the public is at a less infinite distance, but not sufficiently less for one not to consider all of the rays reflected by the actor (or all the spectators' gazes) as parallel. And for all intents and purposes each spectator sees the mask in a *consistent* manner with differences which are surely negligible—compared to the idiosyncrasies and attitudes which may be grasped in various ways and about which it is impossible to generalize—and which moreover are neutralized in a crowd behaving as a flock, that is as a crowd.

By means of slow head movements up and down and lateral rotations, the actor shifts the shadows on the surface of his mask. And experience has shown that the six principal positions (and a like number of less clearly established positions for the profile) suffice for all expressions.[119]

*Sound.* "It goes without saying that the actor ought to have a special *voice* which is the voice of the role, as though the mouth cavity could never emit anything save what the mask itself would say if its lip muscles worked. And it is better that they do not work and that during the entire play the speech delivery be monotonic." [120]

Jarry was not only preoccupied with the specifics of a total theater; he had a number of acute insights into the general obligation of the dramatist committed to finding the language that belonged strictly to theater in an age whose fashionable dramaturgy consisted largely of adapted novels or staged *trompe-l'œil* glimpses into slices of private life.

The dramatist must think, first of all, in terms of the stage. The amateur or literary dramatist tends to think in terms of what *happened* in the story he is telling, whereas the true dramatist will think of what *is happening* on the stage; and the artistic exigencies of the two approaches are radically different. It is immaterial whether acting or storytelling came first; they have for centuries been disparate. The traditional theater at the turn of the century was literary rather than dramatic, depending primarily on speech and verbalized psychology for its impact rather than on visual and auditory stimuli. In other words, it was cerebral rather than dramatic; and if the cerebral is to be stressed it may surely be stressed better in novels and textbooks than in fleeting dramatic evenings.

Jarry, having rejected the popular theater aimed at the multitude, or what Artaud called "théâtre digestif," [121] is quite clear about his position in this matter: "The only one who ought to write for the theater is the author who thinks first in terms of the dramatic form. One can then derive a novel from his play, should one wish, for one can tell the story of an action; but the reverse is almost never true; and if a novel were dramatic the author would then have first conceived (and composed) it in the form of a play." [122]

The language of the theater, its impact, is visually moving, like Artaud's "animated hieroglyphs": "The theater which animates impersonal masks is only accessible to one who considers himself virile enough to create life: a conflict of passions more subtle than known conflicts or a character which is a new being. Everyone admits that Hamlet, for example, is more alive than the man in the street, for he is more complex, with greater synthesis, and even self-sufficient, for he is a walking abstraction." [123]

The theater, according to Jarry, should hold up to man the mirror that will show him how he is and not how he would like to be. This concept of man and his theatrical double is somewhat similar to that developed by Artaud. Witness the following statement by Jarry:

Once the curtain went up, I wanted the stage before the public to become like that mirror in the stories of Mme Leprince de Beaumont in which the vicious see themselves with bull's horns and a dragon's body, depending on the exaggeration of their vices; and it is not amazing that the public should be stunned by the sight of its ignoble double, which they had never been totally confronted with before; and which is made up, as Catulle Mendès has so well expressed it, "of eternal human imbecility, eternal lust, eternal gluttony, baseness of instinct which takes over completely; of decorum, virtue, patriotism, and the ideal of people who have dined well." Really, there is no point in expecting a funny play, and the masks make it clear that the comic element must at the most be the macabre comedy of an English clown or a dance of the dead. [124]

Artaud produced August Strindberg's *A Dream Play* in the Théâtre Alfred Jarry, [125] but Strindberg's *The Ghost Sonata* is more in keeping with his theatrical concepts. Artaud contended that *A Dream Play* belonged in any respectable theater's repertory, and he had a detailed plan for production of *The Ghost Sonata*.[126] This drama is a mood play in which the mummification of the male at the hands of the female is the persistent, crushing theme.[127]

The action first takes place outside a colonel's elegant home and then in several rooms inside the house. Hummel, an old man in a wheel chair, encounters Arkenholtz, a student who is on his way home from a night of bravery during which he has saved several people in a disaster. Hummel agrees to help the student meet the colonel's daughter. He arranges that Arkenholtz meet the colonel at a performance of *The Valkyrie* and be invited to his home. Both the old man and the student appear to be prescient.

Scene Two: inside the house, Hummel arrives uninvited and sets about stripping the colonel of his falsely assumed name, title, and paternity. He is about to destroy all the guests at the "ghost supper" when the mummy of the girl's once-lovely mother and the servant Bengtsson divulge Hummel's own criminal past. The apparently omniscient and omnipotent Hummel is crushed and is led off, cackling like a parrot, to the closet where the mummy had been sequestered and where a rope is provided for him to hang himself—which he does after a black screen has been placed before the closet door.

Scene Three: the student and the colonel's daughter hold a romantic conversation about nature and the cosmos. Their love is impossible, however, and the girl, who is apparently stricken by what Musset called a "moral illness," dies behind the black screen while Arkenholtz plays the harp and recites a verse. There is a fade-out to a projection of Böcklin's picture, *The Isle of the Dead,* to the accompaniment of melancholy music.

The play is of particular interest to us here, not for the

over-all narrative or the dream-like quality in itself, but rather for several subordinate events and for the prescience of Hummel and Arkenholtz. In Scene One, Hummel says to the student: "If you were a Sunday child, you would see him [the dead consul in a room off the second-story balcony] presently come out of that door to look at the Consulate flag flying at half-mast." And, indeed, a moment later the dead man does just that. A milkmaid appears several times during the play but is invisible to Hummel who in other ways is clairvoyant. She is the incarnation on stage of his crime—the ghost of a girl he drowned to keep secret yet another crime.

The turning point of the play is the moment at the end of Scene Two when Hummel is defeated and the parrotlike madness is transferred from the mummy to him. The third scene would be an anticlimax were it not for the presence of the cook, who is sapping the strength of the household by removing all nourishment from the food. They are aware of what she is doing but are helplessly entranced by some strange spell and can do nothing to avert their subjugation. Thus the power of which Hummel had been temporarily the custodian has not been destroyed with him but goes on into the hands of others, and we the viewers conclude that the fault lies in the human condition and that the mortal sickness pervading the play is universal and is merely exteriorized in Hummel and then in the cook.

The somber dreamlike quality is obviously an extension of Strindberg's mind and its madness and preoccupation with his illegitimacy and, in a vaster sense, of the Scandinavian mentality reflected in the Swedish appreciation of, say, O'Neill's plays and, recently, Ingmar Bergman's films. However, what interests us are the staging effects, notably the effect of the destruction of time and the exteriorization of mental intangibles, regardless of the spirit in which they were conceived.

In an author's note to *A Dream Play,* Strindberg writes: "In this dreamplay . . . the Author has sought to reproduce the disconnected but apparently logical form of a dream. Anything can happen; everything is possible and probable. Time and space do not exist; on a slight groundwork of reality, imagination spins and weaves new patterns made up of memories, experiences, unfettered fancies, absurdities and improvisations." [128]

This note may be applied in many respects to *The Ghost Sonata* as well, for the prescience of Hummel and Arkenholtz contrives to destroy on stage all traditional chronological unity even if we allow for the staging of flashbacks. In addition, the macabre nightmare of the mummy serves as a cathartic of sorts, for, as Strindberg adds in his note, "Sleep, the liberator, often appears as the torturer, but when the pain is at its worst, the sufferer awakes—and is thus reconciled with reality. For however agonizing real life may be, at this moment, compared with the tormenting dream, it is a joy." [129]

Artaud, in his plan for the mise en scène of *The Ghost Sonata*, while definitely retaining the characteristic Artaudian language, echoes Strindberg's remarks concerning *A Dream Play:* "This play evokes a feeling of something which, though not on the supernatural or nonhuman plane, is to some degree part of a certain inner reality. That is its appeal. It manifests only what is known for a fact though it might be hidden or oblique. The real and the unreal are mingled in the play as in the brain of a man who is falling asleep or who awakens suddenly facing in the wrong direction." [130]

The contemporary playwright whom Artaud sponsored with the most enthusiasm was his fellow ex-surrealist, Roger Vitrac, who was his partner in the Théâtre Alfred Jarry. Artaud produced *The Mysteries of Love* in 1927 and *Victor: or, The Children Take Power* in 1928–29.

In the first volume of Vitrac's collected plays there is a note under the list of dramatis personae of the first play which reads: *"Victor* was played for the first time on Monday, December 24, 1928, in Paris, on the stage of the Comédie des Champs-Elysées, by the Théâtre Alfred Jarry. The mise en scène was by Antonin Artaud." [131]

The action of the play takes place on September 12, 1909, in the home of the Paumelles, between 8 P.M. and midnight, and it revolves around two couples, the Paumelles and the Magneaus, and their children, Victor, aged 9, and Esther, aged 6. The occasion is Victor's birthday. Through his quickness of mind and his apparent lacklogic, he not only mystifies his parents and the Magneaus, who are guests for the evening, but also manages to bring out into the open the two scandals of these households: the fact that Charles Paumelle and Thérèse Magneau have for several years been carrying on an affair, and Antoine Magneau's insanity or obsession which centers around the nineteenth-century military traitor, Bazaine, whose story he recites on cue, verbatim, from the *Dictionnaire Larousse.*

With certain peripeties the play discloses the love affair—the news of which Emilie Paumelle receives with feigned indifference—and pursues the mental decline of the brilliant but mad Antoine, who finally hangs himself from a dowel of the sort oilcloth is rolled around, which he has stuck in the flag holder on the Magneaus' balcony—but not before leaving a wordy, hyperelegant suicide note.

Victor also dies, on the ninth anniversary—to the minute—of his birth, a death which he has foreseen. The tragic distance between Victor and his parents and other adults is emphasized when, after having intimated on his deathbed that he understands the *Uniquate,* or the secret of life, he is treated like a baby by the doctor: "Well, well. So here is our little patient. Isn't my little boy feeling well? Does he have an ache in his little tummy?"

In the last scene Victor dies, a black curtain falls, there are

69

two shots, and the curtain rises, revealing the corpses of Charles and Emilie. The maid, Lili, enters and exclaims "Why this is a drama" as the final curtain falls.

It is true that what has taken place is, in fact, a drama or melodrama containing slightly ludicrous exaggerations of the ingredients that went into most traditional plays of the late nineteenth and early twentieth centuries: the theme of adultery, the boudoir crises, and the ultimate killing.[132] Vitrac lampooned these conventions while exploiting them in good antiplay tradition. There are, however, two specific grotesque elements that make this play more than a mere pastiche: namely, the unexpected arrival of Ida Mortemart, a lovely lady who suffers from a chronic disorder that causes her repeatedly to fart, to her humiliation and to the glee of the other characters; and the inordinate growth of Victor, who is over six feet tall and grows during the play, first measuring 185, then 186 centimeters, and finally two meters (six feet, seven inches).

Keeping in mind Jarry's mirror, we, the spectators of *Victor*, are reminded of our horridness not through the only slightly exaggerated behavior of the adults, but through the extremely grotesque exteriorization of Victor's monumental intelligence and the adults' lack of comprehension of it. Not only is Victor taller than the others, he is basically better than the others, whose insignificance is brought home to us by their behavior—which at first seems to outrage the norm of human decency. We quickly realize, however, that they are weak in comparison to Victor, and even compared to Antoine, who is touched with a sort of divine madness. In this play, which is a forerunner of Ionesco, the over-all paradox is that the adults, especially Thérèse, Emilie, and Charles, are so neutral their nothingness is actually made monstrous by comparison to Victor's precocious brilliance.

There are overtones of the dream play in Victor's perception of his own forthcoming death. This sense of portent is

70

rationally inexplicable and must be viewed in the light of the artist's role as a maker of miracles in his own right.

*King Ubu* and *The Ghost Sonata* are archetypes of the modern fantasy theater which in slight variations has been called everything from "surrealist drama" (Apollinaire) to "anti-theater" (Ionesco) and "theater of the absurd" (Martin Esslin). The most important modern movement that consciously endorsed artistic and cultural exploitation of the ludicrous, the grotesque, and the unexpected was the surrealist movement.

Artaud's involvement with the surrealist movement of André Breton and his followers was intense, but of short duration. Artaud was by nature "surrealistic" and embodied what the movement admired when it was formed. Thus he was not profoundly influenced, in the true sense of the word, by surrealism, which, on the contrary, endorsed his personality and predilections.[133]

Artaud's interest in Breton goes back to before the latter's first surrealist manifesto—to 1923, and it continued in 1924. Jean Hort has written:

Lautréamont, Baudelaire, Gérard de Nerval, Rimbaud, Cocteau, the provocative manifestoes of André Breton, the works of Shakespeare, of Edgar Allan Poe, of Gide—these, as well as many other dramatists and writers, were the ones we used to discuss—or rather about whom I used to question Artaud who was already forming a definitive opinion of each.[134]

In 1924 Artaud became a member of the surrealist group, and his collaboration reached its peak when he was extended editorial carte blanche for the third number of *La Révolution Surréaliste* which appeared in April, 1925. The task of editing that issue was consigned to Artaud, although Pierre Naville

71

and Benjamin Péret are still listed as the editors. Artaud composed almost the entire contents of this issue, mostly in the form of anonymous open letters to the Pope, the Dalai Lama, and others. Those who collaborated in the issue, which had as its over-all title "1925: End of the Christian Era" ("1925: Fin de l'ère chrétienne"), were Robert Desnos, Michel Leiris, Jacques Baron, Max Morise, Pierre Naville, Paul Eluard, Giorgio de Chirico, Paul Klee, André Masson, Man Ray, Benjamin Péret, Raymond Queneau, Jacques-André Boiffard, Dédé Sunbeam, Maurice Béchet, and Théodore Lessing. The texts by Artaud are available in a slightly different sequence in his Complete Works.[135]

Artaud was the incarnation of the surrealist ideal. In 1946, after their differences had been healed, Breton was able to write that "Antonin Artaud was, in our day, the one who went ahead the most vigorously in that vein."[136]

Artaud's surrealist years, 1924 to 1927, are described by Breton as follows: "And there was The Nervometer (Le Pèse-Nerfs), and The Umbilicus of Limbo (L'Ombilic des limbes), and the third number of La Révolution Surréaliste, composed completely at the discretion of Artaud who in the pages of that journal reaches the loftiest point of phosphorescence and restores to me the shiver of true life by revealing to me man assaulting the summits toward and against the very lightning."[137]

In 1927, however, Breton's admiration for Artaud's phosphorescence was not great enough to prevent an ideological schism. Breton excluded a number of surrealists, or the heretics withdrew from the group, depending who tells the tale. In any case, Breton's megalomania, which in part led him to form his own post-dadaist group and made him desire to retain total control of it, as well as the political dispute over the group's commitment to communism, caused the ouster of Artaud and

72

other members of the group who had been accused by Breton of deviationism.

The discord in the group had, in 1925, resulted in Breton's seizing full control of *La Révolution Surréaliste*. He prefaced the fourth issue with a note entitled "Why I Have Taken Over the Editorship of *La Révolution Surréaliste*" ("Pourquoi je prends la direction de *La Révolution Surréaliste*"), in which he castigated "Artaud (and, no doubt, Philippe Soupault, Roger Vitrac, Michel Leiris, Raymond Queneau and a few others who were suspected of flirting with the world of letters)." [138] In 1927 Breton, Aragon, Eluard, and Benjamin Péret attempted, in their pamphlet entitled *In Broad Daylight* (*Au grand jour*), to justify their anomalous adhesion to the French Communist party. They were particularly vicious in their attack on Artaud.

In the 1952 radio broadcasts which make up Breton's *Conversations* (*Entretiens*), the head of the surrealists recalled Artaud's dedication to the movement but implied that Artaud's destructive negativism was one of the principal reasons for his expulsion. Referring to the open letters in the third number of *La Révolution Surréaliste*, Breton wrote as follows: "There is something 'verbal' about them, even if the verb or word is very noble and very fine. It is an area of lacunae and ellipses in which I personally no longer feel in communication with the innumerable things which, in spite of everything, I find pleasant and which make me keep my feet on the ground. One too frequently forgets that surrealism *loved* a great deal and that what it scathed with a vengeance is precisely that which thwarts or vitiates love." [139] Breton, forgetting the vitriol of his denigration of Artaud in 1927, would in 1952 have attributed his split with Artaud and others to a highly intellectual philanthropy, claiming that the trance experiments which had gotten out of hand with René Crevel and Robert Desnos [140] frightened

73

him: "Finally, I was leery of a kind of paroxysm which Artaud was certainly headed for—as Desnos had been on another level—and it seemed to me that there was an expenditure of energy on our part which we would be unable to counteract later. In other words, I saw only too well how the machine was working at full capacity but I did not see how it could continue to get fuel." [141]

Artaud retaliated against *In Broad Daylight* within the month with his privately printed brochure, *In the Dark of Night: or, The Surrealist Bluff* (*A la grande nuit ou le bluff surréaliste*). He justified his destructive invective and accused the surrealists of pusillanimity: "That is precisely what makes me puke about surrealism: the contemplation of the innate impotence, the congenital weakness of these gentlemen, compared to their eternally ostentatious attitude, their empty threats, and their blasphemies shouted in a vacuum." [142]

The difference in attitude between the other surrealists and Artaud results, no doubt, from the fact that Artaud made no change in himself, no adjustment, to become "surrealistic"; and when the casuistry of the surrealists changed, Artaud remained the same, only now, in his own words, "these gentlemen have judged my presence among them inopportune." [143]

Artaud blamed surrealism's ideological compromise with communism not only for his disenchantment but also for the demise of the movement: "Moreover, is there still a surrealist adventure, or didn't surrealism rather die the day Breton and his followers felt they had to rally behind communism and to seek in the realm of facts and current events the result of an action which normally could only be got in the intimate framework of the brain." [144]

The new ideological compromise necessitated a certain optimism or love which Artaud was physically incapable of feeling; and his physical, creative, and intellectual activities were always intimately related:

74

I scorn life too much to think that any change whatever that might take place in the realm of appearances might change anything about my hateful condition. What cuts me off from the surrealists is that they love life as much as I scorn it. The wish to rejoice on all occasions and through all pores forms the core of their obsessions. But is it not asceticism that is one with the true magic, even the dirtiest, even the blackest magic? Even the diabolical hedonist has his ascetic side, a certain sense of self-mortification.[145]

Artaud continued to appear from time to time in *La Révolution Surréaliste*, and he was reconciled with André Breton in 1937, but for all intents and purposes his surrealist period ended in 1927 [146]—unless one considers him an archetypal surrealist before, during, and after the movement.[147]

As different as a symbolist play by Maurice Maeterlinck may at first appear to be from a surrealistic play like *King Ubu*, they are both in the lunar tradition. It is significant that Maeterlinck's plays and poems were admired not only by Artaud but also by André Breton, perhaps for their straightforward presentation of prescience and the fact that the plays are full of the mysterious Celtic ingredients of dark forests, grottoes, deep pools, storms, and half-human wraiths.

*Pelléas and Mélisande*,[148] Maeterlinck's most famous play, is a lunar play in which the sparse action is subordinate to the spirit of the play. Golaud finds a lost and seemingly amnesiac girl named Mélisande by a fountain, and brings her home to the castle where Arkël, his father, is ill. Golaud marries the girl who is soon with child. Pelléas, Golaud's brother, loves her as she loves him, but their love remains chaste. However, Golaud is suspicious, and when he finds them by the fountain one night, he wounds Mélisande and kills Pelléas. Mélisande delivers a premature girl and then dies, neither from her minor wound nor from childbirth, but because "she couldn't live.

. . . She was born senselessly . . . to die; and she is dying senselessly."

This play is really a state of mind. It is constructed in light and shade, in chiaroscuro, and the light of the fateful noon hour and the shade of night intermingle in the *décor* and in the dialogue. Mélisande seems less a human being than a water goddess. The sense of fatality that hovers over the play is not allowed to dissipate for an instant. Golaud and Pelléas smell death in the stagnant pool in the nether regions of the castle; Pelléas and Mélisande venture into the grotto by the sea, from which too adventurous souls fail to reappear, and they see three white-haired old people sleeping there; Mélisande loses the ring she received from Golaud in the bottomless pool in the forest, the Fountain of the Blind. The light and dark patchwork is related to the blindness and vision of the characters. We know, from the minute Mélisande drops the ring in the fountain, that there will be a death by drowning. We think it might occur when Pelléas leans over the stagnant pool in the castle, but he ultimately ends up at the bottom of the fountain.

Watery death is characteristic of many lunar plays, especially the symbolist play in which the bottomless nocturnal pool imparts a sense of danger and mystery. The Celtic tone of Maeterlinck's drama is reinforced by the clairvoyance of the characters, notably of Mélisande and of Pelléas' friend Marcellus, who writes to Pelléas that he knows exactly when he will die.

Despite Golaud's actions, the play is essentially static, and its dominant theme is one of crushing inevitability. Lunar plays of this sort differ greatly from solar plays in over-all structure. Whereas solar drama tends to crescendo to the crisis which is followed by a traditionally brief denouement, lunar drama immediately alerts the viewer to the crisis which may even have preceded the drama itself, and the play is the

76

inexorable unwinding or denouement of the action or situation. Thus *'Tis Pity She's a Whore,* without ever resorting to psychological conflict of the sort found in so many plays, yet rises from scene to scene in a crescendo of sheer action, whereas the rhythm of *Pelléas and Mélisande* unfolds in a frighteningly predictable manner.[149]

Antonin Artaud wrote in 1923, in a preface to Maeterlinck's *Twelve Songs (Douze Chansons),* that "the name of Maurice Maeterlinck evokes an atmosphere above all. . . . The unconscious irrevocability of ancient drama has become to Maeterlinck the very *raison d'être* of the action. The characters are puppets manipulated by destiny." [150]

Lunar drama does not depict the imitation of an action that will ideally impart an emotion to the audience; it rather uses the emotion itself as its raw material, much as the impressionist painters tried to work as directly as possible with the attributes of light.

The establishing of a mood, which as far as the symbolists were concerned meant the elimination of traditional narrative action and that ersatz emotion we call suspense, required the adoption of a static force in which "the rhythm is rarefied, spiritual, and we are at the very source of the tempest, in the circles immobile as life." [151] And the static drama retains its sense of restrained violence only as long as it remains in the hurricane's eye.

Artaud believed Maeterlinck to be the first to introduce "into literature the multiple richness of the subconscious" [152] in that he tried to give life to pure thoughts.[153] It was no doubt this aspect of lunar drama that most appealed to Artaud. He felt it portended a new theater and a new aesthetic: "Such thoroughly deep-seated truths are only separated from the superior truths by an invisible membrane which the mind of man shall someday surely pierce." [154] It is ironic and tragic to consider the extremes to which Artaud went in his efforts to transcend this barrier of the id and to relate that transcendency to various vital organs.*

In this first part of the study I have described the major cultural and dramatic influences which contributed to the formation of Antonin Artaud's concepts, or were so compatible with his ideas that he quite naturally turned to them for illustrative material. I cannot hope to have exhausted the many antecedents of Artaud's ideas, but have rather tried to block out in broad strokes the portrait of his "imagined ideal." Further details will be added in Part Two, in which I shall examine Artaud's dramatic ideas themselves.

* For example, see above, pp. 28–29.

# Part Two

## THE

## IDEAS

*  *  *  *  *  *  *  *  *  *  *
  *  *  *  *  *  *  *  *  *  *
    *  *  *  *  *  *  *  *  *

*The Theater and Its Double* (*Le Théâtre et son double*), Antonin Artaud's major theoretical work, to which all his other writings are confirmatory marginalia or addenda, was published by Gallimard in the "Collection Métamorphoses," reprinted in 1944, and re-edited in 1964 by Gallimard in the fourth volume of Artaud's *Complete Works* along with "The Seraphim Theater" and *The Cenci.* In 1966 *The Theater and Its Double* and "The Seraphim Theater" were brought out in a very accessible edition in Gallimard's "Collection Idées."

*The Theater and Its Double* contains an author's preface and thirteen essays, some presented as notes or letters. The table of contents is as follows: "Preface: The Theater and Culture" ("Préface: Le Théâtre et la culture"),[1] "The Theater and the Plague" ("Le Théâtre et la peste"),[2] "Metaphysics and the Mise en Scène" ("La Mise en scène et la méta-

81

physique"),[3] "The Alchemical Theater" ("Le Théâtre alchimique"),[4] "On the Balinese Theater" ("Sur le théâtre balinais"),[5] "Oriental Theater and Occidental Theater" ("Théâtre oriental et théâtre occidental"),[6] "No More Masterpieces" ("En finir avec les chefs-d'œuvre"),[7] "The Theater and Cruelty" ("Le Théâtre et la cruauté"),[8] "The Theater of Cruelty (First Manifesto)" ("Le Théâtre de la cruauté [premier manifeste]"),[9] "Letters on Cruelty" ("Lettres sur la cruauté"),[10] "Letters on Language" ("Lettres sur le langage"), "The Theater of Cruelty (Second Manifesto)" ("Le Théâtre de la cruauté [second manifeste]"),[11] "An Affective Athleticism" ("Un Athlétisme affectif"),[12] and "Two Notes" ("Deux Notes").[13] "The Seraphim Theater" ("Le Théâtre de séraphin")[14] was intended for inclusion in *The Theater and Its Double* and figures in the proposed table of contents in the first of Artaud's two letters to Jean Paulhan dated January 6, 1936. It is not known why it never appeared there.

There are three themes which recur in the tapestry of Artaud's theoretical works: (1) a plea for a new language of the theater; (2) catharsis, incorporating the ideas of cruelty and the double; and (3) the almost mystical sense of vocation which the metteur en scène ought to possess.

Artaud felt that the extant theater, despite certain partial innovations in the first quarter of the twentieth century, was merely disguised naturalism, suffering from dry rot. He felt the need for a completely new approach to the art of the theater and a completely new language belonging to the theater itself, not merely the illusionistic representation of novels or staged dialogues. In "Metaphysics and the Mise en Scène" Artaud asked: "Why is it that in the theater, at least theater as we know it in Europe, or better still, in the West, everything that is specifically theatrical, namely, everything that does not fall under the dictates of expression by the word or by words,

or, if you will, everything that is not contained in dialogue
. . . is left in the background?" [15]

The language for a new theater which Artaud sought must,
he contended, be developed within the stage space itself and
not superimposed on it from a script composed in the den: "I
say that the stage is a physical and concrete place that demands to be filled, and demands that one make it speak its own
concrete language." [16] The language of the stage consists then
of anything that inheres in the stage itself and particularly
anything that the theater can avail itself of which is distinct
from the spoken word; and this language "consists of all that
which occupies the stage, of all that which can manifest and
express itself materially on a stage and which is addressed first
of all to the senses rather than to the mind as is the case with
the language of words." [17]

The language of the stage which Artaud desired was based
primarily on gesture and sound, but it brought into play all the
areas of the stage phenomenon such as *décor*, lighting, and
props. The most specific itemization of recommendations that
Artaud has given us is found in "The Theater of Cruelty (First
Manifesto)." Despite their lack of development in depth, these
recommendations are as close as Artaud ever comes to specify-
ing the nature of his desired language of the stage, and he
frequently intimates these recommendations in his letters and
other essays.

Artaud was not unaware of the frustrating nature of his
truncated elucidations, for in the third of the "Letters on
Cruelty" he wrote: "I lay down rigorous and unexpected principles, grim and terrible in nature, and just when one expects
to see me justify them I pass on to the next principle." [18]

Some sections of the technical recommendations in "The
Theater of Cruelty (First Manifesto)" are vague and offer
little more than a cursory remark, but others actually condense

concepts which otherwise are found only in inflated or fragmentary form in Artaud's theoretical writings.

In Artaud's ideal theater "every spectacle will contain a physical and objective element appreciable to all. Cries, laments, apparitions, surprises, dramatic virtuosities ("coups de théâtre") of all sorts, the magical beauty of costumes based on certain ritual models, splendrous lighting, the incantatory beauty of voices, . . . concrete apparitions of new and surprising objects, masks, mannequins several meters tall, and brusque changes in lighting."[19] The physicality of the stage presentation does not call for the abolition of speech, but rather for its subordination to the over-all production, and even for a new approach to the delivery of lines in the theater: "It is not a question of suppression of the articulated word, but of giving to words approximately the importance they have in dreams."[20]

In Artaud's ideal language of the stage, objects take on mathematical relationships which, though more numerous, are nevertheless reminiscent of Jarry's six positions for mask vectors, and voices and sounds take on a physical dimension like that which Artaud suggested the Balinese dancers were able to create: "Furthermore, there is a concrete idea of music where sounds come into play like characters, where harmonies are cut in half and are mingled in with the precise interventions of words."[21] Musical instruments are also to be objectified on the stage, and one must seek the means of producing new sounds. "They will be used in the capacity of objects and as an integral part of the *décor*.

"Furthermore, the necessity of acting directly and profoundly on the sensitivity through the organs makes it advisable, from the viewpoint of sound, to seek out absolutely new qualities and vibrations of sound, qualities which contemporary musical instruments do not possess."[22]

As there was a need for new musical or sound apparatuses,

so there was a need for new lighting devices, although, due to the variance in sound and light speeds, the invention of machines capable of varying the latter presents greater difficulties than the invention of machines capable of making new sound effects. However, Artaud felt that every effort should be made to seek such lighting novelties: "The illuminating apparatuses currently in use in the theaters are no longer adequate. In view of the specific action of lighting on the mind, effects of luminous vibrations must be sought, as well as new means of projecting lighting in waves, or in sheets, or like a volley of flaming arrows." [23]

Artaud's program calls for a timeless, ritualistic costume in keeping with his earlier suggestions for a hieroglyphic idea of the costume as an abstract reflection of the human being: "one ought to avoid modern dress as much as possible, not in a fetichistic and superstitious predilection for the ancient, but because it is absolutely apparent that certain millennial costumes, ritualistic in function, although they might have been of a given period in history, retain a revelatory beauty and appearance." [24]

Artaud wanted an open-stage effect based on the Kabuki and other oriental theaters, in which the stage would not be the room with three walls of naturalistic, illusionistic theater, but rather spread throughout the theater area—a converted barn, factory hall, or hangar—in the corners and along catwalks against brightly lit walls "whitewashed with the aim of absorbing [sic] the light," the spectator being able to observe the action surrounding him from "mobile chairs which will permit him to follow the performance which will take place all around him." [25] Around the spectator the action would unfold without benefit of décor—or, more accurately, costumes, props, figures, everything would contribute to the effect of the décor: "There will be no décor. That will be adequately taken care of by hieroglyphic actors, ritualistic costumes, mannequins ten meters tall representing King Lear's beard in the storm, musical instruments as tall as a man, objects of unheard-of form and purpose." [26]

Artaud, speaking of the works to be produced by the Théâtre de la Cruauté, writes: "We will not act out written plays, but in and around known themes, facts, or works we will make direct attempts at staging." [27] This anti-text attitude seems to have developed gradually, though Artaud always felt the play ought ideally to be derived on and from the stage space and not from a script. In the early manifesto of the Théâtre Alfred Jarry's first season (1926–27), Artaud writes: "It is quite evident, however, that we will work with established texts; the works that we will put on belong to literature, . . . one thing alone seems invulnerable to us, one thing alone seems true: the text." [28] By the time of composition of the various essays in *The Theater and Its Double,* however, Artaud's antitext concepts were explicit, even if he himself was not to observe them in the one official application of his Theater of Cruelty—his production of *The Cenci.*

Artaud, in the first manifesto of the Théâtre de la Cruauté, gives a list of projected productions to be given over a period of several years by that theater. Anyone familiar with the great changes in the plans of the Théâtre Alfred Jarry, as expressed in the theater's four manifestoes, will realize that if Artaud had had the use of a well-endowed theater he would have been likely to change his projects radically. Whereas Artaud had stated earlier his intention of producing *Woyzeck* first in the Théâtre Alfred Jarry's schedule of performances, he has now relegated that play to a minor spot, saying that it should be produced "in a spirit of reaction against our principles, and as an example of what one can derive scenically from an exact text." [29] Similarly, he later stated his intention of producing *The Conquest of Mexico* as the first production of his Théâtre de la Cruauté, only to renege in favor of *The Cenci.*

Artaud's projected list is interesting for an insight into the several types of drama which could conceivably be adapted to his concept of a Theater of Cruelty. He hoped eventually to put on, among other things, the following items, "without taking the text into account": [30] an adaptation from a work "of Shakespeare's time," perhaps *Arden of Feversham;* [31] a play by Léon-Paul Fargue; a section of the *Zohar* ("The story of Rabbi-Simeon, which has the unstinting violence and force of a conflagration"); [32] the story of Bluebeard ("containing a new idea of eroticism and cruelty"); the sacking of Jerusalem ("with the blood-red color flowing from it"); a story by the Marquis de Sade ("in which the eroticism will be transposed, rendered allegorically, and cloaked in the sense of a violent exteriorization of cruelty"); one or more Romantic melodramas ("in which improbability will become an active and concrete poetic element"); *Woyzeck;* and some Elizabethan plays ("stripped of their texts and of which we will only retain the period trappings, the situation, the characters, and the action"). [33]

The two parts of the stage language that Artaud refers to most frequently in his theoretical writings are those of gesture and sound. He had an idea that words and sounds could be treated in the same spatial manner as gesture, for, as he writes in "Metaphysics and the Mise en Scène," "words, too, have possibilities of sonorization, various ways of being projected in space." [34] Artaud frequently attacked the written play, and the language of the theater he envisioned was to use motion, gesture, lighting, and objects as its basic vocabulary, though not at the expense of words. Words were to be considered less as thought conveyers than as objects in themselves, tonalities, prolonged modulations, yelps, barks, all in harmony or calculated dissonance with the gestures and objects in the stage space. In "Oriental Theater and Occidental Theater" Artaud wrote: "So, to change the destination of the word in the theater one must make use of it in a concrete and spatial sense and, as such, have it combine with everything in the art of the theater that is spatial and of significance in the realm of the concrete; one must manipulate it like an object which is solid and which can move things, first in the air and then in an infinitely more mysterious and secret domain." [35] This objectivization of words and sounds, plus his conviction that eventually there would be devised some means of annotating the new stage language he advocated, helps explain Artaud's varied modulations in his plays—such as the trite love words in the beginning of *The Spurt of Blood* (*Le Jet de sang*)—and the abrupt interpolation into conventional texts of what at first appear to be nonsense syllables:

> lo kundum
> a papa
> da mama
> la mamama
> a papa
> dama
>
> lokin
> a kata
> repara
> o leptura
> o ema
> lema
>
> o ersti
> o popo
> erstura
>
> o erstura
> o popo
> dima [36]

Artaud, in a letter to Henri Parisot dated September 22, 1945, claimed—it would appear irrationally—to have written a book in 1934 which was in an international language and was printed in a small edition and subsequently lost: "Here are some samples of language which the language of that old book must have resembled. But one can only read them in cadence, based on a rhythm which the reader himself must find in order to comprehend and to think:

> *ratara ratara ratara*
> *atara tatara rana*
>
> *otara otara katara*
> *otara ratara kana*
>
> *ortura ortura konara*
> *kokona kokona koma*
>
> *kurbura kurbura kurbura*
> *kurbata kurbata kenya*
>
> *pesti anti pestantum putara*
> *pest anti pestantum putra*

but this is only valid when uttered in an urgent flow ("jailli d'un coup"); picked out syllable by syllable it becomes worthless." [37]

Certain words in these representative texts resemble real words (papa, mama, dama, repara, ortura, kurbura, kenya, anti) and others may be explained in terms of the Artaud mythos (ema, koma, kurbata, pesti, and pestantum),[38] but they are essentially meaningless utterances, objectified word-sounds. Some critics have maligned Artaud for what they feel are irrational paroxysms,[39] but it is evident that Artaud's outbursts are largely based on theoretical convictions, and if there is, indeed, any paroxysm, it appears to be one of frustration at the constricting intellectual slant of conventional words. Words in space, like gestures and objects, are part of the magic of the stage as Artaud points out at the end of "Oriental Theater and Occidental Theater":

> It is in this light of magic use and witchcraft that one must consider the art of staging, not as the reflection of a written text and of all that projection of physical doubles which are given off by the text, but as the burning projection of everything of objective consequence which can be derived from gesture, word, sound, music, and from combinations thereof.[40]

The single ingredient of the stage language which preoccupied Artaud the most was that of gesture and movement on the part of the actors, mannequins, and masked and costumed figures. Referring to the Balinese dancers' stylized, hieratic gestures, he wrote: "It is important to note at the same time the hieroglyphic aspect of their costumes, whose horizontal lines extend in all directions beyond the body. They are like large insects full of lines and segments made to connect them to God knows what perspective of nature, and they no longer seem to be anything but a remote geometry of that perspective." [41] That Artaud eventually hoped this geometry of gesture-perspective might lead to a means of transcription for the new theatrical language is suggested in "The Theater of Cruelty (First Manifesto)," [42] as well as in "On the Balinese Theater," in which he expressed the need to "crystallize a new and, I might add, concrete conception of the abstract." [43]

As Artaud wrote in "On the Balinese Theater," the "concrete poetry" or "poetry in space," whose composition was the ultimate aim of his language of total theater, was to be based on signs which "constitute veritable hieroglyphs in which man, in the sense that he contributes to their formation, is only a form like any other to which, due to his double nature, he does add a certain prestige, however." And it was to be communicated by "gestures and postures having an ideographic value such as those which are still to be found in certain unperverted pantomimes." [44]

Artaud distinguishes between the pantomime of gestures representing words or meaningful phrases, which he considers perverted, and that of gestures which evoke ideas that exist primarily in terms of movement itself. In some fragmentary notes apparently pertaining to "Metaphysics and the Mise en Scène," he distinguishes between the pantomime of mimicry and that of ideography *: "Two types of pantomime, / the ideographic, / and the one in which gestures are nothing more than equivalents to words." [45] Gordon Craig,[46] Etienne Decroux, and the Jean-Louis Barrault of "Around a Mother" ("Autour d'une mère") were champions of the mime that Artaud considered unperverted. Eric Bentley has described the transpositions of Decroux from mimicry into pure mime: "Decroux showed us how he makes each part of the body progressively more independent of the others: we glimpsed the über-marionette [advocated by Gordon Craig] in the process of creation. He gave us an exact imitation of a man planing wood and followed it with the same movement transposed into art by selection and heightening: here was pantomime in the process of creation." [47] Artaud felt that Barrault in "Around a Mother" [48] gave a performance that contained the secret forces which could reach an audience, and he wrote in the final section of *The Theater and Its Double* that

it was there, in that sacred atmosphere, that Jean-Louis Barrault improvised the movements of a wild horse, and that one was suddenly amazed to see him become a horse.

* In view of a forthcoming section on theory, I should like at this point to extend this separation to the Aristotelian distinction between "aping" and "imitation."

His performance proves the irresistible action of the gesture and demonstrates triumphantly the importance of gesture and movement in space.[49]

Artaud's technical suggestions today seem commonplace
enough. Lawrence Wunderlich is able to write about Genet,
Ionesco, and other now-prominent playwrights: "In addition
to language itself, the new playwright has become increasingly
interested in the possibilities of integrating many other kinds
of sound in his work: music, rhythmic effects, the perception
of sounds in nature, animal noises, sounds associated with the
various occupations of human beings, etc." [50] Artaud intimated these ideas as early as 1925 and expressed them more
and more emphatically in the early thirties. His technical
innovations were to some extent limited by adversities—such
as lack of money and hostility from potential backers—which
never permitted him to experiment on the stage, and by the
fact that, as a visionary, he was calling for future changes
based on an idea rather than for changes immediately applica-
ble with extant props and equipment.

Eugène Ionesco feels that Artaud's contribution to the art of
the stage is limited to a few technical remarks, the rest being
the product of a disturbed and morbid mind: "Artaud was a
troubled man, not a desperate man, a temperamental rebel, not
a thinker. His anxiety was convulsive, not at all philosophical.
Yes, except for a few little purely technical observations on the
theater, which have remained valid, the rest is a wind bearing a
slightly nauseating, inconsistent, and infected stench." [51] Although less critical of Artaud's nontechnical ideas, Arthur
Adamov limits his acknowledgment of Artaud's influence to the
physical recommendations concerning the stage space: "It is
Artaud who, with Strindberg—whose *Dream Play*, as you
know, Artaud produced—taught me the primordial role of
the stage space"; [52] and he has renounced the mystical ideas:

"Long ago I was influenced by the 'general' ideas of Artaud, but despite our friendship—and he was a friend—and the admiration I continue to have for him, I no longer can agree with him about the magical reconstitutions which he thought he could produce and impose on the stage." [53]

As limited as Artaud's specific recommendations may be—and it is clear at a glance through *The Theater and Its Double* that the technical observations occupy a small portion of the pages and do not come close to the simplest conjectural theater we might contrive for Artaud from the spirit of the other pages—they all pointed toward an ideal which might well be the ideal of any serious playwright: Artaud hoped to bring about, through his language of the stage space, a change or purgation in the spectator. I should now like to consider this more general preoccupation of catharsis, which is the second recurring theme in Artaud's theoretical writings.

We must consider for a moment Artaud's concepts of "the double" and "cruelty," for these two Artaudian trademarks laid the foundation for his definition of catharsis or purgation of the emotions. Artaud's use of the word "double" in the title of the collected essays indicates its importance in the Artaudian *Weltanschauung*. The multiplicity of the meaning of the word is indicated by Artaud himself in a letter to Jean Paulhan, dated January 25, 1936, and sent from a small North American port, while he was on his way to Mexico, in which he announced his choice of the title for his book:

I think I've found a suitable title for my book.
It will be:

THE THEATER AND ITS DOUBLE

for if the theater is the double of life, life is the double of the true theater, and that has nothing to do with the ideas of

93

Oscar Wilde on Art. This title will correspond to all the doubles of theater which I thought I had found over so many years: metaphysics, the plague, cruelty.

The reservoir of the energies made up of Myths which men no longer incarnate is incarnated in the theater. And by this double I mean the great magic element ("agent") of which the theater, in its forms, is only the figuration while we wait for the theater to become that element's transfiguration.[54]

The double takes many forms, as this quotation reveals, and there are numerous minor, tertiary applications of the word, and several secondary uses of it. It is no doubt related in one capacity to the shadows in Plato's famous cavern in Book 7 of *The Republic*,[55] and in another to Jarry's mirror-play in which the spectator sees himself as the monster he truly is; [56] but the primary underlying meaning of the double is, rather than either of these, a combination of both. Thus the double is itself double as is implied in the remark to Paulhan that if the theater is the double of life, so is life the double of the true theater. If the theater is a mirror held up to life, there are also, simultaneously, shadows cast through and beyond that mirror, and the dramatic event is a continuous interplay between the spectator and the great magic element behind the play itself, of which the play is ideally a transfiguration. This magic element, this double, is the reservoir of the theater and all the arts, for, as Artaud maintains in "No More Masterpieces," "beneath the poetry of texts there is poetry pure and simple, without shape and without text." [57] The revelation of this agent or element to the audience via the dramatic experience would ideally produce the transfiguration of which Artaud speaks. This transfiguration entails, perhaps, an annihilation of the double, and we are confronted with a paradox: the double must become

94

one to give expression to Artaud's ideal "true theater." This paradox is the irreconcilable one at the root of the Artaud mythos: the solar-lunar, Male-Female division of the *princeps*. This division is inherent as well in Artaud's mental condition,[58] and it is reflected in his continual search for unity—frequently through destruction—and in his efforts to "resolve or even annihilate all the conflicts arising from the antagonism of matter and mind, of idea and form, of the concrete and the abstract, and to smelt down all appearances into one single expression which would be like spiritualized gold." [59]

Artaud's binary view of the cosmos is expressed repeatedly in *Heliogabalus: or, The Crowned Anarchist* (*Héliogabale, ou l'anarchiste couronné*),[60] a most interesting work which is as much a spiritual autobiography as it is the historico-legendary account of Heliogabalus it purports to be. The paradox is made more striking by the involute nature of each half of the binary *princeps*. Each half contains the kernel of its opposite like the *yang–yin* symbol.

> There is the sun temple at Emesa which seems to have precedence over the other temples of the male sun, as though there were several suns and each taken separately were the double of the others, and as the moon is the female double of a god which is unique and masculine; and the temple of the sun-moon at Apamea which is fully paved with moonstones; and the temple of the moon at Hieropolis near Emesa which, ostensibly devoted to woman, contains a ragged and puny throne for the male who is only shown once a year in the guise of Apollo.[61]

The intimate connection between the double and cruelty as Artaud ascribes those qualities to Heliogabalus might well be applied to Artaud's own ideas:

A strange rhythm comes into play in the cruelty of Heliogabalus; this initiate did everything with art and in double. I mean he did everything on two planes. Each of his gestures was double-edged.

Order, Disorder,
Unity, Anarchy,
Poetry, Dissonance,
Rhythm, Discord,
Grandeur, Puerility,
Generosity, Cruelty.

From the top of the newly erected towers of his temple to the Pythic god, he threw down wheat and men's members.[62]

The double has, then, a very personal rather than logical place in Artaud's dramatic concepts. Its various radii emanate from the inner core of Artaud the man and not Artaud the rationalist. However, for Artaud, the ultimate goal in the dramatic event is the abolition of distinctions and the uniting of the spectator, the actor, and the mystical realm beyond the scenic event in a transfiguration or purgation—by means of violence if necessary.

No doubt the idea of catharsis is considered consciously or unconsciously by all perpetrators of drama, from tribal dancers to highly sophisticated playwrights like Euripides and Racine, and most theoreticians must be compared to Aristotle whose *Poetics* contains the oldest and best-known description of purgation through a dramatic event. Artaud's concepts to some extent repeat those of Aristotle, but if the ultimate intent is the same, namely catharsis, the means by which Artaud thought catharsis might be achieved differs on several major points from that of Aristotle.

Artaud thought that catharsis might be achieved through a Theater of Cruelty, the germ of which lies in his idea that catastrophes contain a metaphysics linked to the theatrical experience and that catharsis might be induced by the effigy or simulation of disaster on stage: "I propose to return in the theater to that fundamental magic idea, picked up by modern psychoanalysis, which consists of attempting the cure of a patient by making him assume the exterior attitude of the state to which one would restore him." [63] Thus the spectator does not, through some arcane process, see himself as he truly is, but rather sees the mirror image of his true self actually staged, which, by eliminating the psychological or cerebral intermediary of word-meaning, appeals directly to the senses. Artaud felt strongly that purgation must be achieved through the senses (which is not unreasonable since purgation is supposed to be a physical experience) not the mind, using as its language that which is proper to the stage, with as its theme cruelty that is not sadism or morbidity but the emphatic, harshly delineated gesture, the all-out impact action which will evoke a sense of danger, the loss of which he felt had caused the degeneration of the theater in his day.[64] Artaud already knew this "element of uneasiness proper for casting the specta- tor into the desired state of doubt" [65] to be his theoretical goal in the second manifesto for the Théâtre Alfred Jarry, 1926–27.

Artaud felt that cataclysms, such as a plague, were at least in theory beneficent. In an early text from *Art and Death* (*L'Art et la mort*) entitled "The Clear Abelard" ("Le Clair Abelard"), Artaud speaks of establishing a "metaphysics of disaster":

Poor fellow! Poor Antonin Artaud! That's who that impo- tent fellow is who is scaling the stars, who is trying to match his weakness against the cardinal points of the elements, who, with each of the subtle or solid faces of nature, is trying to compose a tenable thought, an image which will stand up. If he could create as many elements, at least

97

provide a metaphysics of disaster, the beginning would be the end! [66]

In an article which appeared in Spanish translation in *El Nacional* of Mexico City in July, 1936, Artaud describes the beneficent effects of destruction in Hinduism: "In India there are worshippers of Shiva, 'the destroyer,' and of Vishnu, 'the conservator.' However, destruction is a transforming force. Life maintains its continuity by means of the transformation of the appearances of being." [67] Artaud also expressed this idea in "The Theater and the Plague": "In the theater as in the plague there is something both triumphant and vengeful. One feels clearly that the spontaneous conflagration which the plague ignites wherever it passes is nothing other than an immense liquidation." [68] Artaud equates the forces of the plague or the cataclysm with those of the theater, not any theater, but "essential theater" or "total theater." The essential play is characterized, as is the plague, by a strange sun of abnormal intensity in whose light the impossible becomes our natural element.[69]

Aristotle suggested that purgation of the emotions be brought about through pity and fear [70] and that such purgation would be possible in a tragedy that is "serious, complete, and of a serious magnitude." [71] Artaud almost paraphrases Aristotle's passage, claiming that the best tragedies are founded on the stories of a few houses and that monstrous familial crimes are situations to be sought by the poet,[72] when he advises the dramatist to seek themes in time-tested myths and declares in "The Theater and Cruelty" that using "famous characters, atrocious crimes, superhuman devotions, we shall try to focus a performance which, without having recourse to the defunct images of the ancient Myths, is capable of extracting the forces that stir in them." [73]

Artaud's ideas seem at first to be very similar to Aristotle's concerning the means of achieving catharsis, notably when we consider such a passage as that of the statue of Mitys in the *Poetics*,[74] which appears to contain seeds of Artaud's metaphysics of disaster, his use of giant mannequins,[75] and his concept of the unexpected event as a means of inducing catharsis. The fundamental differences between the two theories may be attributable in part to the passage of time, which has seen many changes in the approach to the problem of defining surprise, imitation, humor, and what constitutes a complete play.

Artaud's idea of a Theater of Cruelty, which dominated his dramatic concepts in the thirties, did not only allow for the terrible deed and the cataclysmic accident, it provided a place for humor, sometimes of a baser sort, for Artaud felt that the unexpected, the surprise, need not be of a readily discernible design like that obvious in the revenge of Aristotle's statue. He advocated "DESTRUCTION-HUMOR through laughter"[76] and called for "explosive interventions of poetry and humor aimed at disorganizing and pulverizing appearances."[77] That the element of surprise sought by Artaud was not based on design is seen in his admiration for the Marx Brothers: "If the Americans, who thought up this type of film, only wish to consider these films in a humoristic vein, and when it comes to humor to stay always on the simple and comic fringe of the meaning of that word, it is their loss, but we are not thereby prevented from considering the end of *Monkey Business* as a hymn to anarchy and to general revolt, that end which elevates the braying [*sic*] of a calf[78] to the same intellectual rank and which gives it the same quality of lucid grief as the cry of a woman who is frightened."[79]

One of the fundamental differences between Aristotle's and Artaud's ideas is that Aristotle did not feel comedy to be as great as tragedy, and he did not feel that the comic could evoke the same purgative feelings as the tragic. Compare, for example, Artaud's idea of "destruction-humor," and his enno-blement of the cow, with Aristotle's more traditional statement that "Comedy is . . . an imitation of characters of a lower type—not, however, in the full sense of the word bad, the Ludicrous being merely a subdivision of the ugly. It consists in some defect or ugliness which is not painful or destructive. To take an obvious example, the comic mask is ugly and dis-torted, but does not imply pain." [80]

Another fundamental difference is that of the proportion of speech to action.[81] Aristotle's "imitation" of an action appar-ently meant, not representation—a word Aristotle uses in reference to mimicry or aping [82]—but the artistic interpreta-tion of a subject from life or from myths like those he had suggested, for little action occurred on the stage or proscenium in Greek tragedy except that necessary to the actors and that made by the movements of the chorus. Artaud, as I have mentioned, was devoted to an antitext type of drama which depended on the various spectacular elements that inhere in the idea of the theater, as opposed to the novel or the oration. Artaud's concept of the exploitation of the stage space is diametrically opposed to Aristotle's statement that

Fear and pity may be aroused by spectacular means; but they may also result from the inner structure of the piece, which is the better way, and indicates a superior poet. For the plot ought to be so constructed that, even without the aid of the eye, he who hears the tale told will thrill with horror and melt to pity at what takes place. This is the impression we should receive from hearing the story of the Oedipus. But to produce this effect by the mere spectacle is a less artistic method, and dependent on extraneous aids. Those who employ spectacular means to create a sense not of the terrible but only of the monstrous, are strangers to the purpose of Tragedy." [83]

The third recurring theme in Artaud's theoretical writing is almost all-pervasive, and ironically it is the least definable while being the most important for subsequent playwrights. This is the spirit of mission which Artaud not only felt but managed, almost painfully, to communicate through his writings. Artaud has been called everything from a madman to a saint, but whatever the sentiment of the individual who encounters his work, that person must be impressed by the singleness of mind and purpose shown by him over a period of some twenty-five years. His unwavering conviction that the art of the theater is the loftiest of arts and in direct contact with primal forces has lent an aura of aesthetic sanctity and martyrdom to many of the more impassioned but less explicable utterances in *The Theater and Its Double.*

There appears to have been a threshold in the development of Artaud's concepts beyond which the ideas became rarefied. This volatilization was no doubt frustrating to positivists,* but it was accompanied by an incandescence which has continued to inspire playwrights and directors—albeit with extremely diverse results—whereas many of his and others' specific recommendations have either become traditional or proved impractical. As Peter Brook has suggested, "You should take Artaud unadulterated as a way of life, or say that there is something in Artaud that relates to a style of theater." [85]

Artaud's essay "The Alchemical Theater" is a tour de force that imparts a sense of the lofty metaphysical calling he felt was proper to the theatrical event; and it is one of the most beautiful essays in *The Theater and Its Double.* Perhaps this is in keeping with the very message of the essay, which, in advocating an "essential theater," realizes that "philosophi-

---

* As Arthur Adamov has said, "Artaud's theoretical work was completely inspirational. There was something evanescent about his dramatic ideas, and when one approached them, when one thought he had grasped them, they vanished." [84]

cally to analyze such a theater is impossible, and [that] it is only poetically and by wrenching from the principles of all the arts whatever they might possess that is communicative and magnetic that one can, through forms, sounds, music, and volumes, evoke—cutting through all the natural similarities of images and likenesses—not the primordial directions of the mind, which our logical and abusive intellectualism would reduce to useless schemas, but states of such intense acuteness, of such an absolute sharpness, that one might feel, through the tremors of music and form, the subterranean threats of a chaos that is both decisive and dangerous." [86] Unlike such essays as "An Affective Athleticism" and "The Seraphim Theater"—in which the basic recommendations behind the discussions of acupuncture and yoga pertain to breathing exercises and physical fitness as practiced by many actors—"The Alchemical Theater" is metaphysical. However, it may be interpreted analogically in that Artaud attempts to rehabilitate the public image of the much-maligned alchemists, not from a belief that one can make gold from lead, given some as yet undiscovered magical ingredient, but from the belief that the physical quest for purity in the elements was paralleled by a metaphysical quest for truth and light.[87] In the world of the ideal "essential theater" for which the philosophers' stone has not yet been discovered, there is nevertheless that higher quest which parallels it, just as the loftier alchemical quest lay at all times behind the attempts to change base matter into gold. Artaud wrote that "all the true alchemists know that the alchemical symbol is a mirage like the theater," [88] and that "many fail to see how closely the physical symbolism which characterizes that mysterious labor corresponds to a parallel symbolism in the mind, to an enactment of ideas and appearances by means of which all that is theatrical in the theater is characterized and made philosophically recognizable." [89]

The sense of mission Artaud felt and often imparts to his

reader is inextricably tied up with his personal life and his mental health, both of which were—and I use the word advisedly—voracious. In the preface to *The Theater and Its Double*, Artaud speaks of the hunger by which certain self-consuming artists are afflicted, and which we may say gnawed at Artaud himself. He compares it to the baser hunger with which the world is more generally afflicted:

> I consider that the world is hungry, and that it doesn't care about culture; and that one is trying artificially to bring back to culture thoughts which are only turned toward hunger.
>
> The most urgent thing is not so much to defend a culture whose existence never saved a man from the worry of living better and of being hungry, as to extract from what we call culture some ideas whose living force is identical to that of hunger.[90]

If the more immediate need of staving off death by starvation is important, on another level the hunger for an artistic absolute is of great importance if one is to live on a level above that of Catulle Mendès' "people who have dined well." [91] Artaud is uncompromising in his vocation as artist: "I mean that if we must all eat right away, we are even more sorely in need of not wasting on the sole concern of eating right away our simple force of being hungry." [92]

This metaphysical hunger is related to the dichotomy in the theater which was postulated in Part One, in that since Nietzsche declared God to be dead, man has been preoccupied with the void that remained, which man, in his guilt, attempted to hide by various subterfuges [93] and which led him to adopt more fervently either the lunar or the solar demeanor. Claude Vigée writes: "Many modern critics, rightly obsessed with the meaning of Nietzsche's proclamation of the death of

God, have neglected the surviving Christian ethos. But to omit either of these two contrapuntal themes condemns the student of literature to forget the essentially dialectic nature of our active experience, to leave unexplained the permanent contradictions of our poetry, its oscillation between extreme negation and extreme affirmation, between pure nihilism and ecstatic, Dionysian 'Lebensbejahung.' " [94] The metaphysical hunger that characterizes the Artaudian mystique is largely a combination of these elements: the sense of void creates an artistic hunger, and the effort to placate or satisfy the hunger is an assertion.

The general climate of our age—perhaps of all ages as Claude Vigée has suggested—contains these elements, but Artaud appears to have had an even more specific concept of metaphysical hunger, relating it to poets who are diabolical, afflicted, or *maudits,* and to the very self-oriented man of the Romantic movement.[95] The nature of Artaud's metaphysical hunger is not clearly established in the preface to *The Theater and Its Double* but may be determined through examination of several passages in his other writings.

The contrast between "people who have dined well" and the artist consumed by metaphysical hunger is underlined in a letter to Henri Parisot dated September 22, 1945: " 'Jabberwocky' is the work of a man who ate well, and one feels that in this piece. I like poems by the starved, the sick, pariahs, the infected: François Villon, Charles Baudelaire, Edgar Allan Poe, Gérard de Nerval, and poems by those tormented by language who are lost in their writings, and not those who pretend to be lost, the better to display their awareness and their know-how of loss through writing." [96] We see, then, that for Artaud the hunger was not only a requisite to good writing,[97] but it was a state not accessible to all, only to a few dubiously gifted with the necessary malediction.

Despite Artaud's frequent use of words pertaining to sexual

organs, especially in his later poems, the hunger is not related to the sex drive according to the playwright himself, who wrote in a poem published posthumously that "the human body needs to eat, / but who has ever tried other than on the level of sexual life the incommensurable capacities of the appetite?" [98]

*The Theater and Its Double* is devoted largely to outlining the task Artaud sets for the culturally aware person of extracting "from what is called culture, ideas whose living force is identical to that of hunger." [99] Artaud feels that this culture is basic to man and has been obscured by man's artificially self-imposed civilization: "And this faculty [of contemplating our acts and of losing ourselves in considerations of the dreamt-of forms of our acts, instead of being impelled by them] is exclusive to humans. I would even say that it is this infection of the human element that spoils for us ideas which ought to have remained divine; for, far from believing in the supernatural and the divine as invented by man, I think it is the millennia-old intervention of man that has ultimately corrupted the divine for us." [100] This contrast between culture and civilization was succinctly expressed in Artaud's pamphlet called *Letter against the Cabala* (*Lettre contre la Cabbale*):

> Civilization is this,
> culture, that.[101]

If one can make any single generalization about the over-all goal lying behind Artaud's various dramatic theoretical pronouncements, it is the piercing of civilization—or what Artaud calls "syphilization" [102]—to get to the elemental culture, to cease to observe our acts and rather be led by them, for Artaud "envisaged a theater which did not numb us with ideas for the intellect, but stirred us to feeling by stirring up pain." [103] The excrescences or forms of civilization will "fall into oblivion, and the spaceless, timeless culture which is contained in our nervous capacities will reappear with an increased energy." [104]

Artaud's tragedy was that for reasons varying from the fact that he was ahead of his time theoretically to the impetuosity which caused him to alienate potential "angels," [105] he never was to have sufficient time, money, or encouragement to experiment fully with his concepts on the actual stage or to implement more than a few of his many projects.

# Part Three

IMPLEMENTATION—
ARTAUD'S
DRAMATURGY

Concerning the genesis of Artaud's *Correspondence with Jacques Rivière* (*Correspondance avec Jacques Rivière*), a reviewer for the *Times Literary Supplement* has written that "Rivière, rightly enough, saw more talent in the letters than in the poems and eventually published the former. This is possibly a unique instance in literary history of an editor rejecting a creative work and then treating the subsequent correspondence between the author and himself as a valid creation." [1]

If this phenomenon is, indeed, unique to Artaud, it happened to him more than once. The rejection in the twenties of the ostensibly creative work in favor of the letters was paralleled by the acceptance of Artaud, in his later years and after his death, as an important theoretician, while his actual dramatic efforts were held to a minimum by financial and critical adversity (and those few efforts cannot be thought of as a fulfilment of the projected theater of Artaud's dreams). [2]

The difficulties in discussing Artaud's Theater of Cruelty are compounded by the fact that, as Romain Weingarten says of Artaud's work, "it is difficult to speak of a theater that did not take place." [3] We must, therefore, in discussing Artaud's dramaturgy, settle for approximations of an ideal that function less as fulfilments of the ideas than as adjuncts to them.

In this section we shall consider to what degree Artaud put into practice or illustrated his concepts in those of his plays whose texts have survived. Artaud's theoretical output greatly exceeded in bulk his works of application, of which there are scarcely ten items that can one way or another be considered implementation of his dramatic concepts. The following plays or dramatic manifestations were written and/or produced between 1925 and 1948.

*The Spurt of Blood* (*Le Jet de sang*) is a brief surrealistic play reminiscent of Jarry's *King Ubu* and Apollinaire's *Breasts of Tiresias,* published in the *Umbilicus of Limbo* by Gallimard in 1925 but not performed until produced by Peter Brook and his associates in the London Theatre of Cruelty in January, 1964.

*The Philosophers' Stone* (*La Pierre philosophale*), an erotic surrealistic pantomime, first appeared in *Les Cahiers de la Pléiade* in 1949 and bears the date 1930–31.

*There Are No Heavens Any More* (*Il n'y a plus de firmament*) is a script in several movements, with little dialogue, which deals with the impending collision of Earth and Sirius. It is unfinished, the fifth movement never having been written. It was published for the first time in Volume II (1961) of Artaud's *Complete Works.*

*The Conquest of Mexico* (*La Conquête du Mexique*), a project for Artaud's Théâtre de la Cruauté, is printed in part in "The Theater of Cruelty (Second Manifesto)" in *The Theater and Its Double.* The full outline for the play was first published in the double March–April, 1950, issue of *La Nef.*

The play deals with the defeat and death of Montezuma at the hands of Cortez.

*The Cenci* is the only full-length play which Artaud wrote and produced. As described in Part One of this study, it deals with the Cenci legend and was adapted from Stendhal and Shelley. The characters and the poetic spirit of Shelley are followed, but the brutality of Stendhal's more historical account is preserved.[4] The performance was based on a written text which is inconsistent with Artaud's conviction that the text should be minimal and subordinate to the whole dramatic experience.* *The Cenci* was hastily produced in the face of financial difficulties, and Artaud seemed to know that it was not a true implementation of his ideal theater: *"The Cenci, which will be produced at the Folies-Wagram beginning May 6, is still not the Theater of Cruelty but it is a preparation for it."* [5] Except for the first scene, which appeared in the special 1948 Artaud issue of *K, Revue de la Poésie, The Cenci* was unavailable until 1964 when it was printed in Volume IV of the *Complete Works.*

After his release from Rodez in 1946, Artaud returned to Paris where, before his death on March 4, 1948, he gave two performances which were literary events. On January 13, 1947, he held a "Tête-à-Tête with Antonin Artaud" ("Tête-à-tête avec Antonin Artaud") at the Vieux-Colombier, during which he raved through some poems and an explanation of his Mexican "envoûtement" or curse before a thunderstruck audience that included many well-known literary and dramatic figures.[6] A portion of this lecture is reproduced as "And It Was in Mexico . . ." ("Et c'est au Mexique . . .") in *The Tarahumaras.*

On November 28, 1947, Artaud recorded, with Maria Casarès, Roger Blin, and Paule Thévenin, the text of *To Have Done with the Judgment of God (Pour en finir avec le juge-*

* One critic even called Artaud's performance as Cenci verbose.

*ment de Dieu*) for airing on February 2, 1948. On the eve of the broadcast, Wladimir Porché, head of Radiodiffusion Française, banned the broadcast on the grounds that it was obscene and contained passages potentially offensive to a friendly nation.\* A jury of some fifty cultural dignitaries was invited to audit the broadcast, and it agreed that the recording could be aired, but Porché remained steadfast in his refusal. This work, performed with sound effects, shouts, yelps, and "xylophonics," has never been broadcast, but the text was published in 1948.[7]

Besides these plays and related manifestations, Artaud wrote two other plays, *Burnt Belly: or, The Crazy Mother*[8] and *The Torture of Tantalus*,[9] which are lost and about which little is known.

It is generally acknowledged that the early works of the Théâtre Alfred Jarry period are preliminary efforts in which Artaud was feeling his way toward the work of the thirties in a development similar to that of the theories. Unfortunately, just as he never completely formulated his ideal theater in *The Theater and Its Double*, he never completely implemented it in the plays and dramatic events we have just listed. There is a variance of opinion regarding which single Artaudian manifestation came closest to implementing his idea of a Theater of Cruelty. Many maintain that *The Cenci* is the only nominal presentation of that theater. Others—in keeping with the idea expressed by Barrault, Weingarten, and Jean Hort that Artaud actually lived his drama[10]—claim that the 1947 Vieux-Colombier evening was the most authentic manifestation of Artaud's theatrical ideal. Yet others, including Artaud, felt that perhaps the suppressed broadcast of *To Have Done with*

---

\* Artaud's broadcast opens with the claim that the United States has a sperm bank which is kept supplied with specimens taken from matriculating schoolboys and saved for artificial insemination in order to create more soldiers for eventual wars.

*the Judgment of God* was a miniature sample of what the Theater of Cruelty could be.[11]

In *The Theater and Its Double,* Artaud often explains one area in the art of the theater in terms of another: for example, he frequently speaks of sounds in concrete terms. The intermingling of sound, gesture, light, and *décor,* encouraged in the theoretical writings, is called for in the stage directions for many of Artaud's plays. The interdependence of these elements is, if anything, greater in the plays. For the sake of clarity, however, I shall consider *décor,* lighting, sound, gesture, and theme in that order.

There are two dimensions to Artaud's *décors* as far as we can tell from sparse indications: a soaring type of stage set containing a number of levels and reminiscent of Gordon Craig's proposed sets for such plays as *Macbeth* [12] and spasmodic, crepitating motions or qualities for lighting, sound, and gesture.

*The Cenci* calls for "a deep spiral gallery." [13] Pierre Jean Jouve describes the set as follows: "The tragedy is inseparable from its *space.* Balthus [who made the sets] invented, drew, and constructed for *The Cenci* a prodigious space, a *décor* at once interior, symbolic, and italianate, in which everything falls into place in an extreme simplicity and force. The built-up *décor* on which people walk is essentially architectonic and is reminiscent of a gigantic prison-palace by Piranese. . . . Thus there is a scaffolding like a huge ladder and a round column against the sky which raises the Cenci palace to a frightening height." [14] *The Philosophers' Stone* opens its description of the *décor* by calling for a niche cut in a black scenery flat and occupying almost the entire height of the theater.[15] Although there is no stratification called for in the stage sets of *The Spurt of Blood* or *There Are No Heavens Any More,* an unseen superstructure is implied, and much of the action takes place overhead. In *The Spurt of Blood,* for

113

instance, there is a stage direction in which occur a collision of stars and "a series of legs of living flesh which fall along with feet, hands, hair, masks, colonnades, doorways, temples, stills, which fall ever more slowly as though they were falling in a vacuum," [16] and in *There Are No Heavens Any More* the single momentary collision of stars of *The Spurt of Blood* has become the entire subject of the drama, and all the action seems to reflect a more intense and dangerous action occurring above the stage until "everything seems to be sucked up by the sky: noises, lights, voices, up to a dizzying height, to the ceiling." [17] Even in the panoramic *décor* of such a play as the schematic *Conquest of Mexico*, Artaud called for a stepped landscape in which there could take place, "on all levels of the landscape, revolt." [18]

Concerning the color of the *décor*, Artaud indicates various colors as well as black and white, but the recurring image is one of crimson, purple, and blood-red. Artaud claims to have borrowed the red for *The Cenci* from Stendhal,[19] but it is found elsewhere in his plays, notably in the backdrop for *The Philosophers' Stone*, which is a "huge red curtain that falls to the ground and rolls in great folds and that takes up the whole back part of the niche, from top to bottom," [20] and in the range of colors in *There Are No Heavens Any More*, which begins with a transition "from red to crude pink." [21] If red is not stipulated in some of the other *décors*, words like "bloody" impart to the stage directions an implication of the use of red, as in certain passages of *The Conquest of Mexico*. Unlike Gordon Craig, who advised directors to read and reread a text until *its* color came forth from the drama, Artaud seems to bring to the stage *his* color of red with its associations of blood and brutality, as in Act I, scene iii of *The Cenci*, in which the scenery of the banquet room "evokes approximately the Marriage of Cana, but made much more barbaric. Purple curtains wave in the wind and fall back in heavy folds against the

114

walls." [22] The red-curtained niche of *The Philosophers' Stone* where Doctor Pale will operate and where Isabelle will go through erotic humiliation is made more sinister by emphasizing its redness through lighting: "The curtain—violently illuminated from above and below—is cut down the middle; and when it is parted one catches a glimpse of a huge reddish light: that is where the operating room is." [23]

No doubt the color red was aesthetically suited to the type of action-theater Artaud advocated, but it seems that the color, rather than being used with calculation, emanated from the same source as the ideas—from Artaud the man. Artaud's obsession with red and the color red's relation to violence are seen in "Traitor Coleridge" ("Coleridge le traître"), in which Artaud writes: "I say poetry, poetic, - *itic* poetry, beautiful hiccup against a blood-red backdrop, the backdrop condensed poematically, the poematics of the hyperbloody real." [24]

Color changes that played variations on the basic *décor* were feasible with the relatively new projectors which replaced the traditional footlights, and Artaud was far from alone in his conviction that lighting should be at the root of the new theater; but he looked beyond the extant projectors to a time when the vibrating, shredded effect he sought would be technically possible. With the use of high intensity arc lamps and color filters, Artaud's "diapason" of light was possible when he called for "flashes of light whose nature changes, goes from red to a crude pink, from silver to green, then turns white, with suddenly an immense opaque yellow light the color of dirty fog and dust storms"; [25] and even the effect of light cast with "the syncopations of a magnified Morse code" was not impossible. However, it becomes difficult to determine implementation when Artaud becomes interpretive and states, for example, that each "hue will be as complex and as subtle as anguish." [26]

The principal lighting effects Artaud indicates in his stage directions are sudden change and extreme intensity. An example of both, which will give us an idea of these effects and how they might be integrated with conventional props, is found in Act IV, scene ii, of *The Cenci*:

> *A curtain of white drops in front of the scenery and is immediately assailed by light.*
>
> *The fanfare resumes, very near-by and menacing.*

> BEATRICE, *covering her ears :* Enough! Enough! The noise of the trumpet keeps me from breathing.
>
> LUCRETIA: It sounds like the final trumpet.
>
> BEATRICE: Can it already be. . . . But no, it's not possible. Everyone and everything is asleep, everything. It is as though even I scarcely realize what has just happened. It is too soon. Nothing could have taken place.
>
> BERNARDO: Beatrice, there are soldiers, soldiers everywhere. I am afraid for you. You must hide right away. (*He weeps*)
>
> BEATRICE: It is too early to be afraid, Bernardo, but too late to cry over what is done.

> *Beatrice and Bernardo start to go off.*
>
> *Lucretia, who had been going toward the sound of the trumpets, fearfully retreats before a blinding and terrible light which little by little covers the stage.*
>
> *The drop rises in one steady motion. Beatrice, Lucretia, and Bernardo enter into the décor proper at the moment when Camillo, followed by guards and preceded by the gleam from a forest of torches, enters from the opposite side.*[27]

Artaud's instructions concerning the use of lighting are quite limited and repetitious, perhaps since there was no way of producing precisely the flickering, dripping, shredded light he sought and which he admired in Lucas van Leyden's paint-

ing of *Lot and His Daughters,* "that stormy light which over-
flows from between the clouds and randomly sprinkles the
countryside," and "that knot of fire which swirls in one corner
of the sky." [28] Artaud's indications for sound effects and voice
modulations are more thorough still.

As we have seen in the various theoretical writings, Artaud
treats voices not as message conveyers but as instruments and
even as objectified props and gestures: "I perceive of the
diapason of voices and the degree of intonation as constituting
stages or levels and, in any case, as a concrete element having
the same importance as the *décor* or the luminous
diapason." [29] This idea of the physicality of sounds having
levels or stages is suggested in the instructions in *There Are
No Heavens Any More* to introduce sounds which "fall from
very high, then stop short and splash out widely, forming
arches, parasols" [30] in which to sound have been attributed
qualities usually reserved for light and substance. Such directions are perhaps inapplicable, but they help to explain the
motivation behind the suggested distortion of dialogue and
Artaud's unorthodox treatment of voices.

Occidental theater in the naturalistic tradition endeavored
to approximate life in its dialogue with as much selection and
editing and combining as creation. Artaud wished to integrate
the dialogue into the general architectonic scaffolding of the
stage space. In the earliest work, *The Spurt of Blood,* we find a
striking example of what Artaud meant by "levels of sound."
A boy and a girl exchange trite love words, but their dialogue
is highly inflected and their voices repeat the expressions not
in exact repetition but as one might echo middle C with high
or low C or vary it with C sharp:

YOUNG MAN: I love you and everything is hunky-dory.
YOUNG GIRL, *with an intensified tremolo in her voice:*
You love me and everything is hunky-dory.

117

YOUNG MAN, *on a lower note:* I love you and everything is hunky-dory.

YOUNG GIRL, *on a still lower note than his:* You love me and everything is hunky-dory.

YOUNG MAN, *on a shrill, exalted note:* I love you, I am tall, I am clear, I am full, I am dense.

YOUNG GIRL, *on same shrill note:* We love each other.[31]

This early effort is perhaps more silly than dramatic, but what Artaud intended was obviously an incantatory declamation—lines, rhythmic and "scandés," in which new tonalities were sprung from the traditional rhythms of speech by the artificial registers employed. We get a clearer idea of what he intended in the more sophisticated treatment of a speech by Harlequin in *The Philosophers' Stone,* in which detailed instructions for the delivery are printed beside the speech:

The words of Harlequin introducing himself are as follows:

JE VIENS
POUR FAIRE TIRER
DE MOI LA PIERRE
PHILOSOPHALE.*

Increasing silences after each bit of sentence, in a bleating, cadenced voice. A brief pause after: *je viens*—long pause after: *de moi*—still longer pause reinforced by the stopping of gestures on: *phale.*

The tone of a hoarse voice deep in the throat and at the same time high-pitched: the voice of a hoarse eunuch.[32]

There are not a great many stage directions in the script of *The Cenci,* but contemporary accounts and the several exam-

* "I have come to have the philosophers' stone removed from me."

118

ples of voice modulation in the manuscript indicate that Artaud had not abandoned his principles even though the actual text seems quite conventional. In the ambush scene a storm is raging and Artaud brings to bear all the elements of flickering light and sound and of cadenced words in his mise en scène:

> *The storm rages more and more fiercely and, mingled with the wind, one hears voices which pronounce Cenci's name, first on one prolonged, sharp note, then like the pendulum of a clock:*
> CENCI, CENCI, CENCI, CENCI.[33]

Of particular interest regarding this passage is a more detailed variant in one of the manuscripts, which reads:

> *. . . pronouncing the name of Cenci.*
> *As a unit: Cenci,*
> *in two beats: Cen-ci,*
> *like the pendulum of a clock: Cenci-Cenci-Cenci-Cenci.*[34]

The reviews of *The Cenci* were mixed, but most of the critics agreed that the voices of Artaud and his leading lady, Iya Abdy, were most unfortunate. Artaud is described as "shouting his text, as if he were declaiming it in a public gathering, cutting up his delivery with a monotonic choppiness," and as "an execrable actor." [35] Iya Abdy was generously considered to be a stunning woman with a terrible speech delivery.[36] We cannot know to what extent the criticism was that characteristic of the reception given most *avant-garde* work and to what extent it was valid.[37] In any case, Artaud's stilted declamation was undoubtedly intentional, for we have abundant testimony to his brilliance as an actor in roles similar to that of Cenci.[38]

Voice control and projection formed but one aspect of

sound in the Artaudian mise en scène, nor was the voice to be used merely to vary tonalities in conventional speech. The voice was to be used almost as an instrument at times, the actor resorting to shouts, barks, and yelps. On January 25, 1945, *Dimanches-Records* described the forthcoming broadcast of *To Have Done with the Judgment of God* as "a sort of symphony of animal cries for which the poet needed no help from a sound effects man, executing them by the sole means of his vocal cords." [39] *L'Aurore* reported, after the jury had audited the recording, that "in the course of the broadcast, Artaud goes from blasphemy to obscenity—in a jerky, staccato language full of disconnected cries." [40]

At times the voice is used for animal noises as in the following passage of *To Have Done with the Judgment of God:*

> There is in the being
> something particularly tempting for man
> and that something is
> 
> CACA
> 
> (here, a roar).[41]

At other times the words fall into what, for want of a better expression, we might call mouth music—the rhythmic incantation of nonsense syllables similar to the sounds made by some jazz singers to approximate instruments:

> o reche modo
> to edire
> de za
> tau dari
> do padera coco . . .[42]

Artaud did not by any means neglect mechanical methods of producing sound effects. If anything, he seems to have developed to a higher degree the concepts of nonvocal sound in the mise en scène than he did the vocal. Despite the forecast of *Dimanches-Records* that Artaud would use only his vocal cords, there were other methods employed for sound production. Artaud refers to "xylophonics," *Le Franc-Tireur* called the broadcast a "work in four voices against a sonorous background," [43] and *Paris-Presse* wrote that "this black and desperate poem, traversed by upsetting cries and punctuated by a voodoo tom-tom, has what it takes to shake the listener . . . and to offend the most hardened ears." [44]

Artaud used the same words—"jerky," "shrill," and so on—which he used to describe lighting and voice to describe musical or nonvocal sound effects. He favored volume, shrillness, and staccato. In the third movement of *There Are No Heavens Any More,* Artaud has a set of instructions calling for great noise:

> Two tom-toms start to beat. One cavernous, the other very shrill, dissonant.
> To the rhythm of the tom-toms one can hear a formidable chorus which grows louder and says:
> > —He who rises shall be brought down,
> > he who rises shall be brought down.
>
> . . . . . . . . . . . . .
>
> Terrible whistles. Crazy dashing about. The hubbub increases. Policemen run by, but backwards as though being overwhelmed.
> The chants and the racket become terrible. [45]

Volume and shrillness were combined in *The Cenci,* for which Artaud wanted the last scene in the torture chamber to be accompanied by an unbearable noise: "The prison gives off the noise of a factory at peak production." [46] In the same scene Artaud uses a screeching wheel, which produced the intolerable sound so dear to him [47] that he may have meant when he spoke of "sonorous tearing sounds," [48] and which is punctuated with cries:

> *On the ceiling of the theater a wheel turns as on an axis which cuts through its diameter.*
>
> *Beatrice, hung by the hair and pushed by a guard who pulls her arms behind her, walks in the direction that the wheel is turning.*
>
> *After every second or third step she takes, a cry rises with the sound of a windlass, a turning wheel, or shattering beams, coming from different parts of the stage.*[49]

Artaud did not limit his sound effects to the manually produced beat of tom-toms and the screech of metal on metal. He always advocated the employment of new and even as yet uninvented apparatuses in his search for the volume and the variety of effects suitable to his idea of a theater. For his 1935 production of *The Cenci* he used a recently invented musical instrument—an electronic keyboard patented in 1922 and presented publicly in 1928. Roger Désormière, who arranged the music for *The Cenci,* used Martenot waves produced by an instrument which, as one critic said, provided an accompaniment that was "strange and penetrating." [50] Martenot waves were well suited to the Artaudian mise en scène because their range and volume-potential surpassed those of previously known instruments. This electronic instrument had an oscillating keyboard which permitted *vibrati,* and attachments permitting glissandi and volumes ranging from the inaudible to sounds greater than the most powerful playing of a symphony orchestra.[51] The use of this instrument in the production of *The Cenci* incorporated into the mise en scène sounds which Jean Prudhomme of *Le Matin* described as "harshly climbing the radiophonic scale," which "throb, growl, and howl—

without respect for convention—the most unexpected noises which have been made into a score by Roger Désormière." [52]

The actors and props were, according to Artaud's concepts, to move about in, with, and against the *décor*, lighting, and sounds, complementing them—now paralleling them, now contrasting with them. The ideal *décor* would, in any still photograph, have the ingredients Artaud so admired in Lucas van Leyden's painting of *Lot and His Daughters:* the high escarpment, the staged bridge, the flickering fire, catastrophic shipwreck, the contrast of action and stillness (the hulls seemingly frozen forever in the middle of their descent to the bottom of the sea), and the sense of danger and latent violence which pervades the group of figures in the foreground, in which there is "an idea of sexuality and reproduction." [53]

The over-all effect sought by Artaud was one in which the stage or the whole theater would be exploited by the furious interplay of all the previously considered aspects of theater art, with the manipulation of oversize props, gigantic masks, strange costumes, and the movements of the actors, as though the van Leyden painting were to spring to life. The intimacy between Artaud's concept of gesture and his concepts of lighting and sound is shown clearly in this passage from "On the Balinese Theater": "For us Europeans what is striking and disconcerting is the admirable intellectuality which one feels crackling everywhere in the tight and subtle nexus of gestures, in the infinitely varied modulations of the voice, in that sonorous downpour like an immense forest which violently shakes itself dry, and in the tracery of movements which is sonorous, too." [54]

Artaud's *There Are No Heavens Any More* contains a scene in which people "pass by in every direction, but of the trains, the subway, and the cars one sees only the shadows on a huge white wall. Moving groups form and patterns appear in these groups, diverse and contradictory movements like an anthill seen from up high," [55] and, in the midst of an infernal noise and frantic movements,

> a woman waves her arms, a man falls, another sticks his nose in the air as though he were sniffing, a dwarf in the foreground runs about like a leaf.
>
> A hysterical woman voices her lament and makes motions of undressing. A child weeps with huge and terrible sobs. . . .
>
> Multiple trampling, a whirlwind begins.
>
> The people who shout are all alone.
>
> No one touches them.
>
> Immense gesticulation.
>
> Sudden stop. Everything begins again. Everyone regains his place as though nothing had happened.
>
> The intersection again begins to swarm with activity.[56]

*There Are No Heavens Any More* is in many ways an elaboration of *The Spurt of Blood* in which there are harbingers of the action of the characters and the manipulation of objects later found in other plays: "The thunder rages, with lightning bolts which zigzag in every direction, and in the zigzags of lightning one can see all the characters who begin to run about, embrace each other, fall on the ground, get up again and run about like fools." [57]

In *The Cenci* the actions of the characters are less surrealistic, more closely related to the action of the play. In the ambush scene there is once again the ominous storm, which never ceased to fascinate Artaud, and in the midst of the thunder and lightning "one can see the forms of the assassins rush forth like tops and pass in front of one another in the light of the lightning flash. At the same time two enormous pistol shots are heard." [58] Throughout *The Cenci* there are many highly stylized gestures, such as Lucretia recoiling be-

124

*Lot and His Daughters,* by Lucas van Leyden, *ca.* 1509. In the Musée du Louvre, Paris. Courtesy Musée du Louvre and Musées Nationaux.

fore the advancing torchlight, Beatrice sliding along a wall, and Cenci drinking blood from a skull,* and we are reminded of the blood-drinking scene in Seneca's *Thyestes,* of Artaud's interest in one day producing some Romantic melodramas, and of his admiration for the Marx Brothers.

The other principal movement on stage is that of objects. In the early works we have the seemingly irrational profusion of sundry objects such as those that fall from the sky in *The Spurt of Blood,* and the unrealistic use of mannequins as in *The Philosophers' Stone* when Isabelle pulls the effigy of Doctor Pale from under her skirts when she has been caught making love to Harlequin.[60] Perhaps these incidents have some symbolic value, but it is difficult to disentangle the elements true to Artaud's concepts from those which seem to derive from his association with the surrealists.[61]

The use of objects and the objectification of the actors (their manipulation as, or with—not merely in front of—objects) seem to take on a more purposeful dimension in Artaud's later dramatic efforts, notably in *The Cenci* and in *The Conquest of Mexico.*[62] In these plays the objects and objectified characters seem less gratuitous, more intimately associated with exteriorization and representation of inner values and emotions. The costumes move as inanimate doubles in harmony with the figures. Artaud is quoted in an article by Marcel Idzkowski in *Le Jour* as follows: "Balthus made the sets and the costumes and in them he stressed the symbolic side—even down to the colors—which I had tried to make apparent."[63] The intimacy of the connection between costumes and living actors who function dually as people and objects in *The Cenci* was noted by Jouve: "Against that tall backdrop, the costumes, whose matter is on the contrary brilliant and lively, caused some amazement without that 'living'

* The reviewer in *Le Journal* wrote that Cenci "even drinks the simulated blood of his children out of a molded cardboard skull."[59]

matter ever upstaging the other one—the dead matter of stones, stairs, gables, portals, wheels, and ropes." [64] Symbolic exteriorization in the costumes and *décor* of *The Cenci* is demonstrated by the costume worn by Count Cenci: a tightly fitted costume upon which the pectoral, abdominal, and leg musculature is outlined in white so that Cenci's tortured inner nature is revealed in the flayed effect of his outer appearance.[65] Artaud himself indicated his interest in symbolization by gesture and composition in "On the Balinese Theater"; and in an interview in *Comœdia* he claimed that in *The Cenci* "one will find a whole experiment of symbolic gesticulation, for the gesture can be symbolic, like the word, in addition to which it has a hieroglyphic sense." [66]

The symbolism of the stage action is perhaps most evident to us today in *The Conquest of Mexico,* perhaps in part due to the fact that it survives not as an annotated dialogue like *The Cenci* but rather in the form of a scenario. This four-act play deals with the defeat of Montezuma, his abdication and murder, and the massacre of the Spaniards. *The Conquest of Mexico,* Artaud affirms, "will put on the stage not men but events presented with an eye to their multiple and most revelatory points of view." [67] The various elements of sound, lighting, and rhythm which characterize the Artaudian mise en scène are again abundantly present, but what is of special interest in this scenario is the direct exteriorization of the underlying idea of the story. As Artaud says of Montezuma's conflict, "one can show almost pictorially, or at least objectively, his struggles and his symbolic discussion with the visual myths of astrology." [68] There are two incidents in particular that call for a physical representation of an abstraction, and they are both most interesting in that they herald the objectification and proliferation which have become the trademarks of the work of Eugène Ionesco.[69] First there is a scene in which the strange duality of Montezuma's personality and his indecision are shown by division of the stage character and a multiplicity of hands and eyes: "Montezuma himself seems cut in half, becomes double; with cutouts of himself dimly illuminated; others blinding with light; with multiple hands protruding from his robes, with eyes painted on his body like a multiple self-awareness, but all questions asked pass from the interior of the consciousness of Montezuma into the crowd." [70] The other example is the proliferation of Cortez: "Strange couples appear, Spaniards on Indian women, horribly enlarged, swollen and black, and sway like two-wheeled carts bent on showing their bottoms. Several Hernando Cortezes enter at the same time, a sign that there is no longer a leader." [71]

In all of Artaud's mises en scène for his own plays, the gestures, symbolic and direct, are combined with motion and sound and light swirling about the entire stage or theater space, with an eye to reaching the senses, the very nerves of the viewer. The same cruelty as that found in the blinding light and the deafening sound should be expressed through the impulse and recoil of the actors. Indeed, the impression one has of Artaud's ultimate goal in many of his scenes is that he wishes to bring to life the suspended animation of the storm and the stilled destruction of the van Leyden painting, which is unmistakably called to mind yet again in *The Conquest of Mexico:*

> Everything trembles, moans like a display rack being abnormally knocked about. A landscape which feels the storm coming: objects, musical effects, cloth, lost robes, and shadows of wild horses pass through the air like distant meteors, or lightning on the mirage-laden horizon, while the wind slants down, vehemently, toward the ground in a light that heralds rain or creatures; then the whole lighting system whirls into action; corresponding to the squealing

conversations and to the quarrels of all the echoes of the population, we have the mute, withdrawn, disconsolate confrontation between Montezuma and his priests gathered in a synod, the signs of the zodiac, the stern shapes of the firmament.

On Cortez' side there is a *décor* of seas and tiny battered caravels and Cortez and his men bigger than the ships and as firm as rocks.[72]

The goal of all this frenzied activity was to force the spectator to realize that "space and time form an affective reality." [73]

I have spoken of the various elements of Artaud's mise en scène and should like to conclude with some remarks concerning the themes he preferred to adopt for his own plays. Artaud once said: "[*The Cenci* will contain] an element of fatality, the symbolic side of the characters will be very clean-cut and I am trying to give the theatrical performance the aspect of a devouring hearth." [74] "Fatality," "danger," and "destination" are three expressions he has repeatedly used to describe the implacable tragic rhythm he strove to achieve by various means, but with his metaphysics of disaster always in the background. The cruelty of action is at times physical, as when Doctor Pale dismembers Harlequin in *The Philosophers' Stone*, but that is superficial, for by cruelty Artaud meant a metaphysical experience shared by the actor and the viewer, and not morbidity or sadism as such. Artaud averred in "No More Masterpieces" that "we are not talking about that cruelty which we can exert on one another by cutting up each other's bodies, by sawing at our personal anatomies." [75] Lionel Abel claims that the difficulty of "most dramatists trying to produce tragedy is not so much to create a sympathetic victim as to create a sympathetic executioner" [76]; but for Artaud it is less a question of sympathy than of extramoral identification

128

through the senses with an aesthetic action that takes hold of us physically, kinesthetically, for, as he said,

> in my performance I try to put the spectator in the middle of the action. . . . The spectator will be surprised by this sonorous displacement and, if his nerves are active, what a magnificent possibility of making him participate in an action whose mise en scène will be regulated by scenic, we might almost say dynamic means, for in the theater we must recover the notion of a kind of direct language between gesture and thought.[77]

Artaud felt that destruction is a transforming force and that cruelty, which is synonymous with the sense of "destruction-humor," is a means of transforming the audience. He describes the extramoral effects of cruelty in connection with the production of *The Cenci:*

> My heroes . . . dwell in the realm of cruelty and must be judged outside of good and evil. They are incestuous and sacrilegious, they are adulterers, rebels, insurgents, and blasphemers. And that cruelty in which the entire work is bathed does not only result from the bloody story of the Cenci family, since it is not a purely corporal cruelty but a moral one; it goes to the extremity of instinct and forces the actor to plunge right to the roots of his being so that he leaves the stage exhausted. A cruelty which acts as well upon the spectator and should not allow him to leave the theater intact, but exhausted, involved, perhaps transformed! [78]

As I indicated in Part One, Artaud was interested in plays in both the solar and the lunar tradition. His own drama, however, is almost exclusively solar. Calamity, destruction, and relentless cruelty are found in all the plays, from *The Spurt of Blood* to *The Cenci*, and the major works unfold around a central diabolical or cursed figure who asserts himself by apotheosizing his evil or by pursuing his task in the face of dissidence: Cenci, Heliogabalus, Cortez, Montezuma, Van Gogh, and Atreus. Artaud wrote of his major dramatic conception, Count Cenci: "In *The Cenci* the father is a destroyer. And that is how this subject goes back to the Great Myths." [79] Even when there is resignation in the plays of Artaud, it is not what we have defined as lunar, but rather the consequence of self-destruction. Thus, Van Gogh, in Artaud's poem-essay, *Van Gogh, Society's Suicide* (*Van Gogh, le suicidé de la société*), [80] turns his solar vision inward and kills himself. The duality of the solar man who contains the seeds of resignation is seen most clearly in the case of Montezuma:

It seems possible to reveal in him two characters:

1. The man who obeys in an almost saintly way the orders of destiny, who passively, and armed with all his faculties, accomplishes the fatality that ties him to the stars. . . .

2. The torn man who, having gone through the external gestures of a rite, having accomplished the rite of submission, wonders inside himself if, by chance, he hasn't made a mistake, and rebels in a sort of superior tête-à-tête around which the ghosts of being hover. [81]

The similarities between Artaud's descriptions of Montezuma and Heliogabalus are striking. The pseudo-historical account of the brutal Roman emperor was written shortly after *The Conquest of Mexico*, and many of the theatrical preoccupations of Artaud's peak dramatic years (1933–35) are reflected in this work.

In selecting great tragic figures from the past as the basis of his major plays and other nondramatic works like *Heliogabalus* and *Van Gogh,* Artaud may have been taking his own advice to found a theater on the great figures and myths of the past, as well as Aristotle's advice to the poet to choose as his subject houses of great suffering.* But behind each legendary figure we detect a shadow, double, or alter ego—Antonin Artaud—whether the figure be the incestuous Cenci, the psychiatrist-hounded Van Gogh, the schizophrenic Montezuma, or Heliogabalus, who upon becoming emperor became Aurelius Antoninus, and who, according to Artaud, "perhaps transformed the Roman throne into a stage." [83]

I have stated elsewhere in this study that I would not consider in depth the concept of the double in connection with Artaud's mental condition; and yet it seems that Artaud is no exception to the generalization that most serious writers write about themselves. It may well be that he never wrote his ideal tragedy—having lived it—but he left behind in his theoretical writings and plays, as well as in his poems, the fragmentary script of a man's struggle to unite himself, in order, like the gods in *Heliogabalus,* "to be done with that separation of the dual beginning, to eliminate its essential antagonism." [84]

Artaud once wrote that "Theater of Cruelty means a difficult and cruel theater first of all for myself," [85] and at the expense of learning how to write perfectly coherent and harmonious poems, as Jacques Rivière had encouraged him to do, Antonin Artaud lived out his tragedy to become one of literature's children of the sun.

---

* Artaud writes of Heliogabalus' lineage that "it would be difficult to find in all of history a more perfect collection of crimes, turpitudes, and cruelties than that of this family." [82]

131

# NOTES

## PREFACE

[1] Bettina Knapp, "An Interview with Roger Blin," *Tulane Drama Review* 7, no. 3 (Spring, 1963) : 113.

[2] James W. Fernandez, "Principles of Opposition and Vitality in Fang Aesthetics," *Journal of Aesthetics and Art Criticism* 25, no. 1 (Fall, 1966) : 53–54.

[3] Denis Diderot, "Paradoxes sur le comédien," in *Œuvres esthétiques*, ed. P. Vermière (Paris: Garnier Frères, 1959), p. 317.

## INTRODUCTION

[1] I have, throughout this study, based my biography of Artaud on the following: Marie-Ange Malaussena, "Notes bio-bibliographiques," *La Tour de Feu*, no. 63–64 (December, 1959), pp. 79–82; Paul Arnold, "Note biographique," in *Lettres d'Antonin Artaud à Jean-Louis Barrault* (Paris: Bordas, 1952), pp. 139–49; Paule Thévenin, "1896–1948," *Cahiers de la Compagnie Madeleine Renaud—Jean-Louis Barrault*, no. 22–23 (May, 1958), pp. 17–45; Paule Thévenin, "Antonin Artaud dans la vie," *Tel Quel*, no. 20 (Winter, 1965), pp. 25–40; and the valuable notes that accompany the texts of the volumes which have appeared to date of Antonin Artaud, *Œuvres complètes* (Paris: Gallimard, I: 1956; II–III: 1961; IV–V: 1964; VI: 1966; VII: 1967).

[2] Artaud, *Œuvres complètes*, I, 21 (see note 1, above). Hereafter referred to as *Œuvres*.

[3] *Ibid.*, I, 20.

[4] *Ibid.*, I, 30.

[5] Ado Kyrou, *Le Surréalisme au cinéma* (Paris: Arcanes, 1953), pp. 187–88.

[6] *Œuvres*, II, 38–39.

[7] *Ibid.*, IV, 389.

[8] Thévenin, "Antonin Artaud dans la vie," p. 37.

[9] *Ibid.*, p. 34.

## PART ONE: ANTECEDENTS

[1] Kurt Seligman, *The Mirror of Magic* (New York: Pantheon, 1948), p. 123.

[2] Sigmund Freud, *Totem and Taboo* (2d printing; New York: Random House, 1961), pp. 29–30.

[3] "Préface d'André Breton," in *Œuvres complètes* by Lautréamont (Paris: Corti, 1953), p. 42.

[4] Antonin Artaud, *Œuvres complètes* (Paris: Gallimard, 1956–67), V, 274. Hereafter referred to as *Œuvres*.

[5] *Ibid.*, V, 280–81.

[6] *Ibid.*, V, 281.

[7] *Ibid.*

**133**

[8] Theodor-Wilhelm Danzel, "The Psychology of Ancient Mexican Symbolism," in *Spiritual Disciplines: Papers from the Eranos Yearbooks*, "Bollingen Series XXX," vol. 4 (New York: Pantheon Books, 1960), 110–11.

[9] Danzel, "The Psychology of Ancient Mexican Symbolism," p. 110.

[10] For an account of such a nocturnal peyote ritual or communion, see anthropologist J. S. Slotkin's account of an Indian peyote meeting of the Native American Church of North America, in *The Drug Experience*, ed. D. Ebin (New York: Orion Press, 1961), pp. 237–69.

[11] André Malraux, *La Tentation de l'occident* (Paris: Grasset, 1926), *passim.*

[12] Ezra Pound, *ABC of Reading* (Norfolk, Conn.: New Directions, n.d.), p. 21.

[13] Paris: Arcanes, 1953. The miraculous discovery of these notes by Berna and a ragpicker has led some to suspect a hoax. The hand is apparently that of Artaud, but the story of how Berna came to possess them is unverifiable.

[14] "Le Mexique et la civilisation," in *Vie et mort*, p. 47. Despite Serge Berna's classification of this text under the heading "Writings in Mexico" ("Ecrits au Mexique"), this opening passage appears to have been written before Artaud's departure for Mexico.

[15] Paule Thévenin to the author, from Paris, dated August 5, 1964.

[16] Danzel, "The Psychology of Ancient Mexican Symbolism," p. 102.

[17] *Ibid.*, p. 106.

[18] Laurette Séjourné, *Burning Water: Thought and Religion in Ancient Mexico* (New York: Grove Press, 1960), p. 112.

[19] *Les Tarahumaras* (Décines, Isère: L'Arbalète, 1955), p. 205.

[20] *Ibid.*, p. 204.

[21] "La Montagne des signes," in *Les Tarahumaras*, p. 45.

[22] See Manuel Cano de Castro, "Rencontre d'Artaud avec les tarots," *K, Revue de la Poésie*, no. 1–2 (June, 1948), pp. 119–23.

[23] "La Danse du Peyotl," in *Les Tarahumaras*, p. 75.

[24] This definition of culture is similar to the Jungian idea of the destruction of animistic projections which obscure the prime syzygic collective unconscious from which they emanate. Thus, to be cultivated is the opposite of being civilized, for then one is encumbered by false projections or forms. Although it is impossible to eliminate the projections, to strive in that direction is laudable: "As we know, it is not the conscious subject but the unconscious which does the projecting. *Hence one encounters projections, one does not make them.* The effect of projection is to *isolate the subject* from his environment, since instead of a real relation to it there is now only an illusory one. Projections change the world into the replica of one's own unknown face. In the last analysis, therefore, they lead to an autoerotic or autistic condition in which one dreams a world whose reality remains forever unattainable. The resultant *sentiment d'incomplétitude* and the still worse feeling of sterility are in their turn explained by projection as the malevolence of the environment, and by means of this vicious circle the isolation is intensified." (C. G. Jung, *Psyche and Symbol: A Selection from the Writings of C. G. Jung*, ed. V. S. de Laszlo [Garden City, N.Y.: Doubleday, 1958], p. 8.)

[25] "Le Théâtre & les Dieux," in *Les Tarahumaras*, pp. 202–4.

[26] Artaud was convinced that he had been hexed by the Indians on a mountain as he tried to reach their demesne. He describes his experience in "And It Was in Mexico . . ." ("Et c'est au Mexique . . ."), and the physical pain in which the alleged curse placed Artaud is described in "The Peyote Dance" ("La Danse du Peyotl"). It is significant that the account of the pain greatly resembles Artaud's 1925 "Description of a Physical State" ("Description d'un état physique") which admittedly concerned his mental illness. The vividness and tenacity of Artaud's hallucinations are evident from André Breton's note in *The Key to the Fields* (*La Clé des champs*): Artaud was convinced that Breton had "lost his life trying to come to his aid" when Artaud was in the hospital at Le Havre in October, 1937, after his ill-fated pilgrimage to Ireland. Artaud was almost as persistent in this hallucination as he was in his conviction that he was under a curse: "I believe, since you have said it to be so, that indeed in October, 1937, you were not at Le Havre but at the Galerie Gradiva in Paris. I maintain that I have never been delirious, never lost the sense of reality, and that my memories, at least what is left of them after fifty comas, are real." (André Breton, "Hommage à Antonin Artaud," *La Clé des champs* [Paris: Editions du Sagittaire, 1953], pp. 85–86.)

[27] Artaud is primarily concerned with the function of gestures. For a subjective description of the hallucinations induced by peyote, see the accounts by Havelock Ellis and Aldous Huxley in *The Drug Experience*, pp. 223–36; pp. 270–74.

[28] "Le Rite du Peyotl chez les Tarahumaras," in *Les Tarahumaras*, p. 10.

[29] In *Pour en finir avec le jugement de Dieu* (Paris: K Editeur, 1948), pp. 15–18. This text is also reprinted in the 1955 *Les Tarahumaras* which contains as well a longer, more detailed account of this rite that is, however, less dramatic. The longer "Tutuguri" is of special interest in that it is dated February 16, 1948, or just a few weeks before Artaud's death.

[30] "Le Rite du Peyotl," in *Les Tarahumaras*, p. 36.

[31] *Ibid.*, p. 26.

[32] *Ibid.*, p. 27.

[33] "At every turn in the road one can behold trees *intentionally* burned in the form of a cross or in the form of beings, and often these beings are double and they face one another, as though to manifest the essential *duality* of things; and I have seen that duality traced back to its beginnings in a sign in the form of ⊖ enclosed in a circle, which I once saw branded on a tall pine." ("La Montagne des signes," in *Les Tarahumaras*, pp. 47–48.)

[34] "Une Race-principe," in *Les Tarahumaras*, p. 64.

[35] "La Danse du Peyotl," in *Les Tarahumaras*, p. 73.

[36] *Ibid.*

[37] *Ibid.*, p. 74.

[38] *Ibid.*, p. 75.

[39] "Préface," *Le Théâtre et son double*, in *Œuvres*, IV, 18.

[40] *Œuvres*, III, 303–4.

[41] *Lettres d'Antonin Artaud à Jean-Louis Barrault* (Paris: Bordas, 1952), p. 97. A few pertinent but inconclusive notes are published in the *Complete*

*Works* under the title "Concerning a Lost Play" ("A propos d'une pièce perdue") (*Œuvres*, II, 185–91). See also *Œuvres*, II, 279, n. 76.

[42] *Œuvres*, II, 185.

[43] *Ibid.*, II, 187.

[44] Aristotle *Poetics* 13.5. All quotations from Aristotle are taken from *The Poetics of Aristotle*, ed. S. H. Butcher (3d ed.; London: Macmillan, 1902).

[45] Aristotle *Poetics* 14.3–4.

[46] "Thyestes seduced Aërope, the wife of Atreus, and was in consequence banished by his brother: from his place of exile he sent Plisthenes, the son of Atreus, whom he had brought up as his own child, in order to slay Atreus, but Plisthenes fell by the hands of Atreus, who did not know that he was his own son. In order to take revenge, Atreus, pretending to be reconciled to Thyestes, recalled him to Mycenae, killed his two sons and placed their flesh before their father at a banquet. Thyestes fled and the sun turned back in horror, and the Gods cursed Atreus and his house." (Sir William Smith, *Smaller Classical Dictionary* [New York: E. P. Dutton, 1958], p. 51.)

[47] *Œuvres*, III, 304.

[48] *Ibid.*, II, 189.

[49] *Ibid.*, II, 185–86.

[50] Seneca, *Thyestes*, trans. and ed. M. Hades (Indianapolis and New York: Bobbs-Merrill, 1957), pp. 20–21.

[51] Delivered at the Sorbonne on December 10, 1931 (*Œuvres*, IV, 345, n. 1).

[52] *Ibid.*, IV, 41–42.

[53] *Ibid.*, IV, 43.

[54] *Ibid.*, IV, 42.

[55] *Ibid.*, II, 19.

[56] *Ibid.*, II, 29–30.

[57] *Ibid.*, IV, 37.

[58] *Ibid.*

[59] *Ibid.*, IV, 344, n. 1.

[60] *Ibid.*, IV, 35.

[61] Havelock Ellis, ed., in John Ford, *Five Plays* (2d printing; New York: Hill and Wang, 1960), p. 86.

[62] *Œuvres*, IV, 36

[63] Henri Martineau, ed., in Stendhal, *Chroniques italiennes* (2 vols.; Paris: Le Divan, 1929), I, xxxi–xxxii.

[64] *Ibid.*

[65] G.-B. Niccolini, *Beatrice Cenci*, in *Opere* (2 vols.; Florence: Le Monnier, 1844), II, 357–448.

[66] Martineau, ed., in Stendhal, *Chroniques italiennes*, I, xxviii.

[67] *Ibid.*, I, 236.

[68] Albert Camus, *L'Homme révolté*, "Collection Idées" (Paris: Gallimard, 1951), p. 69.

[69] Stendhal, *Chroniques italiennes*, I, 239–40.

[70] *Ibid.*, II, 242.

[71] *Ibid.*, p. 249, n. 1.

[72] *Ibid.*, p. 249.

[73] *Ibid.*, p. 252.

[74] *Ibid.*, p. 253.

[75] *Ibid.*, p. 254.

[76] *Ibid.*, p. 260.

[77] John Keats and Percy Bysshe Shelley, *Complete Poetical Works* (New York: Modern Library, n.d.), p. 300.

[78] Sigmund Freud, *Character and Culture*, ed. P. Rieff (New York: Collier Books, 1963), p. 35.

[79] Keats and Shelley, *Complete Poetical Works*, p. 302.

[80] Paul Arnold, "Note biographique," in *Lettres d'Antonin Artaud à Jean-Louis Barrault*, p. 144.

[81] *Œuvres*, V, 268.

[82] *Ibid.*, IV, 96.

[83] It would at first appear that Artaud is referring to the high bridge in the van Leyden painting of Lot and his daughters which he discusses at great length in "Metaphysics and the Mise en Scène" ("La Mise en scène et la métaphysique") and which he says in a letter to Jean Paulhan "is not without resemblance to the Balinese theater" (*Œuvres*, V, 66). Furthermore, Artaud refers to van Leyden as a "primitive." However, several manuscripts and the original *Nouvelle Revue Française* version of the manifesto, which reads ". . . as in certain Persian miniatures or in certain Primitive paintings" (*Œuvres*, IV, 375, n. 27), indicate that Artaud may also have had in mind the architectonic frameworks found in some Persian miniatures or perhaps the balustrades found in the foreground of many Mogul portraits.

[84] *Œuvres*, IV, 115.

[85] Mordecai Gorelik, *New Theatres for Old* (New York: E. P. Dutton, 1962), pp. 54–55.

[86] *Œuvres*, II, 45–46. It is not clear what Artaud meant by Negro-American theater. He does not elaborate here, nor does he mention it elsewhere. In an article entitled "Artaud vu par Blin," in *Les Lettres Françaises* (January 21, 1965, pp. 1, 5), Jean-Pierre Faye tries to link Artaud's ideas to Soviet theater, but Artaud seems to owe no more to it than most of his contemporaries in the theater, and his sympathies appear to be limited to the constructivist *décor*.

[87] This inflexibility in the acting style of Artaud, partly due to a lack of versatility and partly due to stubbornness, was later displayed at Pitoëff's theater. Jean Hort, an actor-colleague of Artaud, tells how Artaud was nicknamed by his fellow actors "the barbed wire actor" and describes his physical articulation as follows: "Whenever Artaud had to move, he stretched his muscles, he arched his body, and his pale physiognomy gave place to a hard face with fiery eyes; in this manner he would advance, manipulating his arms, hands, and legs; and he would zigzag, stretching out his arms and legs and tracing crazy arabesques in the air." (*Antonin Artaud, le suicidé de la société* [Geneva: Editions Connaître, 1960], p. 77.)

[88] *Mr. Pygmalion*, in which Artaud played Pedro Urdemala.

[89] Charles Dullin, "Lettre à Roger Blin," *K, Revue de la Poésie*, no. 1–2 (June, 1948), pp. 22–23.

90 William Butler Yeats, *Essays and Introductions* (New York: Macmillan, 1961), p. 236.

91 Robert Brustein, *The Theatre of Revolt* (Boston and Toronto: Atlantic–Little, Brown, 1964), p. 27.

92 Georg Büchner, *Danton's Death*, in *The Plays of Georg Büchner*, trans. and ed. G. Dunlop (New York: Irving Ravin, 1952), pp. 169–70.

93 Lionel Abel, *Metatheatre: A New View of Dramatic Form* (New York: Hill and Wang, 1963).

94 Büchner, *Danton's Death*, in *Plays of Georg Büchner*, p. 161.

95 *Ibid.*, p. 261.

96 *Œuvres*, III, 229.

97 *Ibid.*, V, 331–32, n. 6.

98 *Ibid.*, V, 33.

99 Earle Ernst, *The Kabuki Theatre* (New York: Grove Press, 1965), p. 88.

100 *Œuvres*, III, 229.

101 *Ibid.*, II, 33.

102 *Ibid.*, II, 46.

103 Donald Keene, *Japanese Literature* (New York: Grove Press, 1955), p. 59.

104 "In October, 1888, Alfred Jarry entered the Lycée at Rennes. His friend and classmate Henri Morin, the younger brother of Charles, handed him the text of *The Poles* [*Les Polonais*], which he put into the form of a comedy that was put on in December, 1888, and in January, 1889, in the attic of the Morin home, and then, after 1890, in the apartment that Alfred Jarry occupied with his mother and his sister Charlotte, using the marionettes of the so-called Théâtre des Phynances. This play, still entitled *The Poles*, is the oldest version of the First Cycle of Ubu, namely *King Ubu*." (Maurice Saillet, ed., in Alfred Jarry, *Tout Ubu* [Paris: Le Livre de Poche, 1962], p. 10.)

105 At the Théâtre de l'Œuvre of Lugné-Poe on December 10, 1896. There was a brilliant group of luminaries involved: "Mise en scène by Lugné-Poe. *Décor* and masks by Pierre Bonnard, Sérusier, Toulouse-Lautrec, Vuillard, Ranson, and Jarry." (*Tout Ubu*, p. 13.)

106 Alfred Jarry, "De l'inutilité du théâtre au théâtre," in *Mercure de France* (September, 1896); reprinted in *Tout Ubu*, pp. 139–45.

107 Alfred Jarry, "Questions de théâtre," in *La Revue Blanche* (January, 1879); reprinted in *Tout Ubu*, pp. 152–55.

108 Alfred Jarry, "Douze Arguments sur le théâtre," *Dossiers Acenonètes du Collège de 'Pataphysique*, no. 5; reprinted *Tout Ubu*, pp. 146–51.

109 Maurice Saillet, ed. "Douze Arguments," in Jarry, *Tout Ubu*, p. 146.

110 Jarry, "De l'inutilité," p. 139.

111 Jarry, "Douze Arguments," p. 148.

112 Jarry, "De l'inutilité," p. 140.

113 *Ibid.*, p. 141.

114 *Ibid.*

115 *Ibid.*

116 *Ibid.*

117 *Ibid.*, p. 142.

118 Jarry, "Douze Arguments," p. 149.

119 Jarry, "De l'inutilité," pp. 142–43.

120 *Ibid.*, p. 143.

121 *Œuvres*, V, 125.

122 Jarry, "Douze Arguments," p. 148.

123 *Ibid.*, p. 149.

124 Jarry, "Questions de théâtre," p. 153.

125 *Le Songe ou le jeu de rêves* was presented by the Théâtre Alfred Jarry at the Théâtre de l'Avenue on June 2 and 9, 1928.

126 See *Œuvres*, II, 113–24.

127 August Strindberg, *The Ghost Sonata*, in *Six Plays of Strindberg*, ed. and trans. E. Sprigge (Garden City, N.Y.: Doubleday, 1955), pp. 263–304.

128 *Ibid.*, p. 193.

129 *Ibid.*

130 *Œuvres*, II, 113.

131 In *Théâtre*, vol. 1 (6th ed.; Paris: Gallimard, 1946), 8.

132 Cf. Wallace Fowlie, *Dionysus in Paris: A Guide to Contemporary French Theater* (New York: Meridian Books, 1960): "In France the supremacy of women's virtue and influence is an important though subtle factor. During the generation preceding the years with which we are concerned [those beginning about 1925], the popular so-called bourgeois play turned almost exclusively on the subject of adultery. Woman was the deceiver and man was the cuckold. Woman was presented as a power unto herself and man as the semi-farcical character who is tricked" (p. 16). Two different, yet basically similar, treatments of this theme which enjoyed great success were Feydeau's *Le Dindon* and Porto-Riche's *Amoureuse*.

133 "His joining with the surrealists, which occurred in fact about 1924, was in no way surprising to those who knew him then. He possessed by instinct (or by artificial acquisition) some of their characteristics: automatic writing under paranoiac stimulus, the dissociation of intellectual faculties and their use in partial synthesis (dream-action, libido-logic, etc. . .). He was already living all that in his daily life of a deranged and drug-addicted man." (Fernand Tourret, "L'Artaud des années mortes," *La Tour de Feu*, no. 63–64 [December, 1959], p. 66.)

134 Hort, *Antonin Artaud*, p. 64.

135 *Œuvres*, I, 252–71.

136 André Breton, "Hommage à Antonin Artaud," p. 84.

137 *Ibid.*

138 Simon Watson Taylor, ed. and trans., "Five Open Letters" by Antonin Artaud, printed in *Encore* 11 (September–October, 1964): 7. Breton mentions only Artaud and Desnos by name (and in another context) in this editorial, but he is obviously unhappy about the preceding issue. He would allay the violence of its invective and remind the group's friends that it is not a negative group. One of Breton's parting shots is obviously directed at Artaud: "Even should the scope of the surrealist movement suffer from it, it

seems to me absolutely necessary to open the columns of this review only to men who are not seeking a literary alibi. Without resorting to ostracism, I nevertheless insist on avoiding at any cost a repetition of the little acts of sabotage which have already occurred in the midst of our organization." (*La Révolution Surréaliste*, no. 4 [July, 1925], p. 3.) One might add that the worst sabotage Breton could imagine was the undermining of his own authority; and he himself proved adept at sabotage on many occasions, notably at Artaud's production of *A Dream Play*, when Breton is said to have shouted disparaging remarks during the play and, with his friends, so disrupted the first performance that the second had to be canceled (see *Œuvres*, II, 265–68).

139 André Breton, *Entretiens, 1913–1952* (Paris: Gallimard, 1952), p. 110.

140 For an account of these incidents, see *ibid.*, pp. 89–91.

141 *Ibid.*, p. 110.

142 *Œuvres,*.I, 284, n. 1.

143 *Ibid.*

144 *Ibid.*, I, 284.

145 *Ibid.*, I, 286.

146 The official obituary was written by André Breton in 1930 in the *Second Manifesto of Surrealism* (*Second Manifeste du surréalisme*) : "That is why I promised myself, as you will note in the preface to the new edition of the first *Manifesto of Surrealism* (1929), to abandon quietly to their sad fate a number of individuals who seemed to me to have justified, such action: that was the case with MM. Artaud, Carive, Delteil, Gérard, Limbour, Masson, Soupault, and Vitrac, named in the 1924 *Manifesto*, and a few others since then." (Breton, *Manifestes du surréalisme* [Paris: J.-J. Pauvert, 1962], p. 160.)

147 Artaud was familiar with German expressionist cinema and admired Conrad Veidt's performance in *The Cabinet of Doctor Caligari* (Hort, *Antonin Artaud*, p. 67), but, despite certain Artaudian similarities to works by various expressionist dramatists (e.g., Hasenclever's telegraphic style minimizing speech and Oskar Kokoschka's violence), despite a mutual admiration for Strindberg, and despite Artaud's collaboration with the expressionist-turned-surrealist, Yvan Goll, I have found no conclusive evidence that Artaud was influenced by the German expressionist theater, if indeed that theater had any identity in the twenties.

148 Maurice Maeterlinck, *Pelléas et Mélisande*, in *Théâtre* (31st ed.; Brussels: Paul Lacomblez, 1912), II, 1–113.

149 The inexorable progression of an expected action characteristic of lunar drama as seen in Maeterlinck, Synge, or Lenormand, is a modern concept, distinct from the tradition of the Greek chorus, but it is supported as early as Diderot: "Unlike most who have written on dramatic art, I am so far from feeling that it is necessary to conceal the denouement from the spectator that I would not consider it beyond my ability to undertake a drama in which the denouement would be announced in the first scene and in which I would even exclude the more violent interest from the circumstances of its revelation." (Denis Diderot, "De la poésie dramatique," in

*Œuvres esthétiques*, ed. P. Vermière [Paris: Garnier Frères, 1959], pp. 226–27.)

[150] Artaud, preface to *Douze Chansons* by Maurice Maeterlinck, Collection "Les Contemporains" (Paris: Stock, 1923) ; reprinted in *Œuvres*, I, 343–44.

[151] *Œuvres*, I, 346.

[152] *Ibid.*

[153] Artaud a few years later described the 1927 production of Vitrac's *The Mysteries of Love* (*Les Mystères de l'amour*) as an "ironic work which concretized on the stage the anxiety, the twin solitude, the criminal ulterior thought, and the eroticism of lovers. For the first time a *real dream* has been produced in the theater" (*Œuvres*, II, 38).

[154] *Ibid.*, I, 347.

## PART TWO: THE IDEAS

[1] It is not known just when Artaud composed his preface, but the nature of the preface indicates that he had either arrived in Mexico or was at least steeped in his Mexican studies when he wrote it. The remarks in Artaud's letter to Paulhan of January 25, 1936 (*Œuvres*, V, 272–73), appear to be a summary of the ideas in the preface, or a prospectus for it, and I would conjecture that the preface was written within some months before or after that letter.

[2] Text of a lecture given by Artaud at the Sorbonne, April 6, 1933, and first published in the *Nouvelle Revue Française* issue of October 1, 1934 (*Œuvres*, IV, 344, n. 1).

[3] Text of a lecture delivered at the Sorbonne, December 10, 1931, and first published in the *Nouvelle Revue Française* issue of February 1, 1932 (*Œuvres*, IV, 345, n. 1).

[4] "The Alchemical Theater," written at the request of Jules Supervielle for the Argentinian review *Sur*, appeared in Spanish in that magazine's issue for Autumn, 1932, and, although the article bears a date line "Paris, September, 1932" (*Œuvres*, IV, 355, n. 1), the period of gestation and composition presumably goes back to the period of February to May, 1932, since Supervielle wrote to Artaud on May 18, 1932, mentioning the completed text (*ibid.*, IV, 421), and Artaud drafted a letter to Supervielle dated March 17, 1932, which contains many of the ideas of "The Alchemical Theater" (*ibid.*, IV, 293). The opening section of Artaud's drafted letter offers an explanation of why he frequently conceived articles in letter form, as with "Letters on Language" ("Lettres sur le langage") : "Permit me to address my article to you in the form of a letter. That is the only way I am able to combat an absolutely paralyzing sense of gratuitousness and to make the point that I have been thinking about for more than a month." (*Ibid.*, IV, 293.)

[5] The first part of "On the Balinese Theater," which ends with the words "et qui était le plus bel ornement de l'une des premières pièces jouées par le Théâtre Alfred Jarry" (*Œuvres*, IV, 68), was published in the *Nouvelle Revue Française*, October 1, 1931, under the title "The Balinese Theater at the Colonial Exposition" ("Le Théâtre balinais, à l'exposition coloniale") (*ibid.*, IV, 355), and the Collette Allendy manuscript bears the date

"Tuesday–Wednesday, 11–12 August, 1931" (*ibid.*, IV, 358, n. 18). The second part of "On the Balinese Theater" is made up of various letters, notes, and fragments pertaining to the Balinese theater and to Artaud's general theories. We do not know exactly when Artaud attended the Balinese theater, but it is likely that it was in late July, as the first reference to it is in a document dated August 2, 1931 (*ibid.*, III, 218). The fire that destroyed the Dutch pavilion did not damage the Bali theater, and the dances went on ("Holland Salvages Relics," *New York Times*, June 30, 1931, p. 8).

[6] Text mentioned by Artaud in three letters to Jean Paulhan written between December 29, 1935, and January 6, 1936 (*Œuvres*, IV, 370, n. 1).

[7] Text first mentioned by Artaud in January, 1936, but probably composed in the last months of 1933 (*ibid.*, IV, 371, n. 1).

[8] Text mentioned in the second letter to Paulhan of January 6, 1936 (*ibid.*, V, 270–71).

[9] First published in the *Nouvelle Revue Française*, October 1, 1932.

[10] These letters, like those on language, are mentioned in the two letters to Paulhan of January 6, 1936. They grew out of correspondence with Paulhan and others, in which Artaud attempted to clarify, or at least to reassert, his ideas expressed in the first manifesto for his Théâtre de la Cruauté.

[11] Published by Editions Denoël (Fontenay-aux-Roses, 1933) in a sixteen-page brochure (*Œuvres*, IV, 378).

[12] With "The Seraphim Theater," this essay was destined for publication in *Mesures* (*ibid.*, IV, 385), but it never appeared there.

[13] The first note, "The Marx Brothers" ("Les Frères Marx"), was published under the title "The Marx Brothers at the Pantheon" ("Les Frères Marx au cinéma Panthéon") in the film column of the *Nouvelle Revue Française*, January 1, 1932. The second note, "Around a Mother" ("Autour d'une mère"), a eulogy of a mimodrama or "dramatic action" by Jean-Louis Barrault based on Faulkner's *As I Lay Dying*, was published in the same magazine, July 1, 1935.

[14] "The Seraphim Theater" was published by Bettencourt in 1948 in the "Collection l'Air du Temps" in an edition of 250 (*Œuvres*, IV, 388, n. 1) and published shortly thereafter with Artaud's "The Eighteen Seconds" ("Les Dix-huit Secondes"), "The Philosophers' Stone" ("La Pierre philosophale"), and "Where Things Stand Now" ("Là où j'en suis") in *Les Cahiers de la Pléiade* (Spring, 1949), 113–39.

[15] *Œuvres*, IV, 44–45.

[16] *Ibid.*, IV, 45.

[17] *Ibid.*, IV, 46.

[18] *Ibid.*, IV, 137.

[19] *Ibid.*, IV, 111.

[20] *Ibid.*, IV, 112.

[21] *Ibid.*, IV, 113.

[22] *Ibid.*

[23] *Ibid.*, IV, 114.

[24] *Ibid.*

[25] *Ibid.*, IV, 115.

[26] *Ibid.*, IV, 116–17.

[27] *Ibid.*, IV, 117.

[28] *Ibid.*, II, 17–18.

[29] *Ibid.*, IV, 119.

[30] *Ibid.*, IV, 118.

[31] Artaud made a great effort to get André Gide to collaborate with him in his projected theater, intending at one time to open with an adaptation by Gide of *Arden of Feversham* (*ibid.*, V, 120–21). Gide was interested in Artaud's ideas but was unwilling to abide by them himself and the project fell through.

[32] Artaud later denounced the cabala and the *Zohar* in most vitriolic terms in his *Letter against the Cabala* (*Lettre contre la Cabbale*).

[33] *Œuvres*, IV, 118–19.

[34] *Ibid.*, IV, 46.

[35] *Ibid.*, IV, 87.

[36] Antonin Artaud, "Chiote à l'esprit," *Tel Quel*, no. 2 (Summer, 1960), p. 4.

[37] Antonin Artaud, *Lettres de Rodez* (Paris: GLM, 1948), pp. 17–18.

[38] *Koma* is intimately related to the shock treatments Artaud received which induced comas; *pesti* and *pestantum* bring to mind Artaud's frequent references to the plague, notably in "The Theater and the Plague"; *kurbata* may relate to the words "courbé," "courbature," and especially to "courbette," which Artaud uses in describing the dramatic ritual of the peyote dance in *The Tarahumaras*; and Artaud gives his own etymology for *ema:* "For *after*, say 'poematic,' after comes the time of the blood. Since *ema*, in Greek, means blood, and since po-ema must mean

afterwards

the blood,

the blood afterwards." (Antonin Artaud, "Coleridge le traître," *K, Revue de la Poésie*, no. 1–2 [June, 1948], p. 93.)

[39] Speaking of the second quotation above, Jean Hort writes that the texts are "interspersed with invented words relating to an incantatory rhythm which has as its motive no concrete idea" (Jean Hort, *Antonin Artaud, le suicidé de la société* [Geneva: Editions Connaître, 1960], p. 126).

[40] *Œuvres*, IV, 88. Further testimony of what Artaud meant by language which had to be "scandé," and by the intimate relationship between sound and gesture in his dramatic concepts is seen in this account by Paule Thévenin of Artaud's method of composition in the later years at Ivry, which indicates that Artaud had his own very vital system of metrics, for "while he was working . . . he would strike a block of wood with an enormous hammer or knife," and at times he "accompanied his work with rhythmic humming, in a language all his own" ("A Letter on Artaud," *Tulane Drama Review* 9, no. 3 [Spring, 1965]: 106).

[41] *Œuvres*, IV, 77.

[42] *Ibid.*, IV, 112.

[43] *Ibid.*, IV, 77.

[44] *Ibid.*, IV, 48.

45 *Ibid.*, IV, 289.

46 There are many similarities between the ideas of Artaud and Edward Gordon Craig concerning the metaphysical *décor*, the nonverbal play, and the marionette. Artaud may have received certain of Craig's ideas directly; or they may have been handed down by Dullin, Copeau, Barrault, and others; or the similarities may be coincidental or attributable to the climate of the theater in the twenties and thirties which Craig helped to create. The only reference to Craig that I have found in Artaud's writing is a brief passage in an article written in Mexico for *El Nacional*, in which Artaud recognizes Craig's undeniable historical importance but appears unimpressed by the Englishman's ideas: "In Seneca's *Medea* as interpreted by Margarita Xirgu they have hung up three moldy dust cloths which supposedly evoke gigantic mountains. And to top it all off, these mountains are stylized. I can't swallow this stylization based on dirty dust cloths. It was Gordon Craig who invented the system in Europe. But we in Europe have already been swamped by these stylizations à la Gordon Craig." (Artaud, "Una Medea sin fuego," reprinted in *México*, ed. Luis Cardoza y Aragón [Mexico City: Universidad Nacional Autónoma de México, 1962], pp. 55–56.)

47 Eric Bentley, *In Search of Theater* (New York: Vintage Books, 1959), p. 176.

48 The editor of the *Complete Works*, who prefers to remain anonymous, writes: "It was from *As I Lay Dying* by William Faulkner that Jean-Louis Barrault derived this 'dramatic action.' The sets and the costumes were by Labisse, the music by a Mexican composer named Tata Nacho. There were only four performances of this play at the Théâtre de l'Atelier: June 4–7, 1935." (*Œuvres*, IV, 385.) Barrault has written about the circumstances of preparation and presentation of "Around a Mother" in his *Réflexions sur le théâtre* (Paris: Jacques Vautrain, 1949), pp. 41–53.

49 *Œuvres*, IV, 169. Artaud ends his note with reservations ("And if one can make a criticism of his gestures, it is that they give us the illusion of a symbol, whereas they were delineating reality; and that is why their action, no matter how violent and active it became, in the last analysis contains no projection" [*ibid.*, IV, 170]), but in the first of his January 6, 1936, letters to Paulhan, Artaud suggests that the Marx Brothers and the Barrault pieces be accompanied by this note: "The films of the Marx Brothers exploded like bombs; but, as with fireworks, their flash quickly disappeared. On the other hand, the show of J.-L. Barrault seems to have truly changed something in the minds of those present." (*Ibid.*, V, 268–69.)

50 Lawrence Wunderlich, "A Playwright's Microcosm," *Chelsea*, no. 16 (1965), p. 60.

51 Eugène Ionesco, letter to the author, dated Paris, October 19, 1964.

52 Arthur Adamov, letter to the author, dated Paris, October 31, 1964.

53 *Ibid.*

54 *Œuvres*, V, 272–73.

55 Artaud refers briefly to this passage of *The Republic* in a simile in "Metaphysics and the Mise en Scène": ". . . where people parade in single file like the Ideas in Plato's cavern" (*ibid.*, IV, 43). In addition, the

following passage from Artaud's preface to *The Theater and Its Double* is characteristic of a number of definitions of the double which mention shadows: "Every true effigy has its shadow which is its double; and art falls as soon as the sculptor who is modeling thinks he has liberated a sort of shadow whose existence will shatter his repose.

"Like every magic culture revealed by appropriate hieroglyphs, the true theater has its own shadows; and, of all the languages and all the arts, it alone still has shadows which have broken through their limitations." (*Ibid.*, IV, 17.)

⁵⁶ Artaud writes in "The Theater and the Plague": "the action of the theater, like that of the plague, is beneficent, for by forcing men to see themselves as they are it causes the mask to fall and uncovers falsehood, cowardice, baseness, and hypocrisy." (*Ibid.*, IV, 39.)

⁵⁷ *Ibid.*, IV, 94.

⁵⁸ The psychiatric interpretation of the double has been the subject of several studies. The various diagnoses which we have of Artaud, following physical and mental examinations at psychiatric institutions, are quite specific in finding him to be a man suffering from a split personality, whose illness had reached an advanced hallucinatory stage (André Bonneton, *Le Naufrage prophétique d'Antonin Artaud* [Paris: Henri Lefebvre, 1961], pp. 45–53). In a more recent study, *Artaud et son double* (Périgueux: Pierre Fanlac, 1964), Dr. J.-L. Armand-Laroche writes: "His body type, which we can picture thanks to an abundant iconography, may be classed as ectomorphic, as is the case with 47% of the schizophrenics. Finally, giving due credit to the theory of predisposing factors, the information we have on his childhood reveals him to be schyzothymic, withdrawn in character, hypersensitive, and inclined to impulsive reactions" (p. 59). Since this aspect of the double is physical and biological and not conceptual, we shall not consider it further in this study. Those interested in more information are referred to Bonneton and Armand-Laroche as well as to Otto Hahn, "Portrait d'Antonin Artaud," *Les Temps Modernes*, no. 192 (May, 1962), pp. 1592–1619; no. 193 (June, 1962), 1854–82.

⁵⁹ *Œuvres*, IV, 63.

⁶⁰ Antonin Artaud, *Héliogabale, ou l'anarchiste couronné* (Paris: Denoël et Steele, 1934) ; reprinted in *Œuvres*, VII, 9–143.

⁶¹ *Œuvres*, VII, 30.

⁶² *Ibid.*, VII, 127–28.

⁶³ *Ibid.*, IV, 96.

⁶⁴ *Ibid.*, IV, 51.

⁶⁵ *Ibid.*, II, 17.

⁶⁶ *Ibid.*, I, 137.

⁶⁷ "La Cultura eterna de México," in *México*, p. 77.

⁶⁸ *Œuvres*, IV, 33.

⁶⁹ *Ibid.*, IV, 37.

⁷⁰ Aristotle *Poetics* 6. 2–3. All quotations from Aristotle are taken from *The Poetics of Aristotle*, ed. S. H. Butcher (3d ed.; London: Macmillan, 1902).

[71] *Ibid.* 6. 2.

[72] *Ibid.* 14. 3–4.

[73] *Œuvres*, IV, 102.

[74] "But again, Tragedy is an imitation not only of a complete action, but of events terrible and pitiful. Such an effect is best produced when the events come on us by surprise; and the effect is heightened when, at the same time, they follow as cause and effect. The tragic wonder will then be greater than if they happened of themselves or by accident; for even coincidences are most striking when they have an air of design. We may instance the statue of Mitys of Argos, which fell upon his murderer while he was a spectator at a festival, and killed him. Such events seem not to be due to mere chance." (Aristotle *Poetics* 9. 11–12.)

[75] The only thing that approaches Aristotle's statue is Artaud's abstract idea in "No More Masterpieces" that his concept of cruelty is not the customary one, but "that much more terrible and necessary one which things can exert upon us. We are not free. And the sky can still fall on our heads. And theater is meant first of all to teach us that" (*Œuvres*, IV, 95).

[76] *Ibid.*, IV, 108.

[77] *Ibid.*, IV, 149–50.

[78] Artaud describes this moment in "Metaphysics and the Mise en Scène": "In a Marx Brothers film, a man who thinks he is embracing a woman receives in his arms a cow instead, which lets out a moo. And through a combination of factors which it would take too long to explain, this mooing, at that moment, assumes an intellectual dignity equal to that of any woman's cry." (*Ibid.*, IV, 52.)

[79] *Ibid.*, IV, 167–68.

[80] Aristotle *Poetics* 5. 1.

[81] Artaud's admiration for the ancients was based on the visual effects of the chorus's movements and the primal quality of the stories. It must be remembered that Artaud, when considering the adaptation of plays from the past, intended to exploit the stories, "stripped of their text, of which only the period trappings, the situations, the characters, and the action would be retained" (*Œuvres*, IV, 119).

[82] Aristotle *Poetics* 26. 1.

[83] *Ibid.* 14. 1–2.

[84] Discussion with author, Paris, June 18, 1963.

[85] Peter Brook *et al.*, "Marat / Sade Forum," *Tulane Drama Review* 10, no. 4 (Summer, 1966) : 226.

[86] *Œuvres*, IV, 61.

[87] *Ibid.*, IV, 60.

[88] *Ibid.*, IV, 59.

[89] *Ibid.*, IV, 60.

[90] *Ibid.*, IV, 11.

[91] Alfred Jarry, "Questions de théâtre," in *Tout Ubu*, ed. M. Saillet (Paris: Le Livre de Poche, 1962), p. 153. For the full quotation, see p. 65 of the text.

[92] *Œuvres*, IV, 12.

[93] Claude Vigée, "Les Artistes de la faim," *La Table Ronde,* no. 112 (April, 1957), p. 43.

[94] Claude Vigée, "Metamorphoses of Modern Poetry," *Comparative Literature* 7, no. 2 (Spring, 1955): 98.

[95] "Artaud introduces into the theatre the feverish intoxication of the *poètes maudits,* Baudelaire, Rimbaud, Lautréamont. Like theirs, his poetic ecstasy is very close to madness." (Robert Brustein, *The Theatre of Revolt* [Boston and Toronto: Atlantic–Little, Brown, 1964], p. 363.)

[96] Artaud, *Lettres de Rodez,* p. 15.

[97] Artaud's sincerity in this matter made Jacques Rivière's advice strike an ironic note when he wrote to Artaud that "with a little patience, even if it means only the simple elimination of digressive images or features, you will succeed in writing perfectly coherent and harmonious poems" (*Œuvres,* I, 22–23).

[98] Antonin Artaud, "Le Théâtre de la cruauté," *84,* no. 5–6 (1948), p. 122.

[99] *Ibid.,* IV, 11.

[100] *Ibid.,* IV, 13.

[101] Antonin Artaud, *Lettre contre la Cabbale adressée à Jacques Prevel* (Paris: Jacques Haumont, 1949), no pagination.

[102] *Ibid.*

[103] Julian Beck, "Thoughts on Theater from Jail," *New York Times,* February 21, 1965, sec. 2, p. 3.

[104] *Œuvres,* IV, 15.

[105] A typical example is Artaud's insulting his potential backers at a reading of *Richard II* which he gave at the home of Lise Deharme, January 6, 1934. See Thévenin, "1896–1948," *Cahiers de la Compagnie Madeleine Renaud—Jean-Louis Barrault,* no. 22–23 (May, 1958), p. 34; and Youki Desnos, *Les Confidences de Youki* (Paris: Arthème Fayard, 1957), pp. 176–78.

## PART THREE: IMPLEMENTATION

[1] "Saint Artaud," *Times Literary Supplement,* March 18, 1965, p. 214.

[2] Paul Arnold writes: "Had Artaud been supported by 'angels'—and the idea is inconceivable—had he been the son of a wealthy man—and, incidentally, who started the unconfirmed legend of a rich and greedy family?—had he had the time and the means to pursue his endeavors instead of, like Gordon Craig, having to stick to written protests, he would no doubt have quickly transcended the purely theatrical element of his Theater of Cruelty. No doubt he would have led us further into that Promised Land which he glimpsed in his conscience." (Paul Arnold, "L'Univers théâtral d'Antonin Artaud," in *Lettres d'Antonin Artaud à Jean-Louis Barrault* [Paris: Bordas, 1952], pp. 45–46.)

[3] Romain Weingarten, "La Force d'un peu plus vivre," *Cahiers de la Compagnie Madeleine Renaud—Jean-Louis Barrault,* no. 22–23 (May, 1958), p. 149.

[4] Artaud's play retains the Cenci characters and the sequence of events of Shelley's play; the principal differences in the texts are that Artaud's is not

in verse and that he actually stages the failure of the hirelings to assassinate Cenci on his way to his country fortress (Act III, scene ii), whereas the same incident is narrated in Shelley's play. For an account of the differences, see Artaud, *Œuvres*, IV, 390–91.

[5] *Œuvres*, V, 45.

[6] According to those present, "Artaud held the stage for three hours, oscillating, apparently, between genius and madness" ("Saint Artaud," *Times Literary Supplement*, p. 214). André Gide, who was present, wrote of the event with enthusiasm: "Artaud's lecture was more extraordinary than one could imagine. It was of a nature never before heard or seen and which will never be seen again. I have retained an indelible memory of it: atrocious, painful, and at moments almost sublime." ("Extrait d'une lettre d'André Gide à Henri Thomas, communiqué par Pierre Loeb," *Cahiers de la Compagnie Madeleine Renaud—Jean-Louis Barrault*, p. 126.) Gide's enthusiasm may also be judged by his alleged behavior at the event. According to a notice under the heading "Lectures" ("Les Conférences"), in *Paru*, Gide "during the intermission climbed onto the stage with an astounding agility to embrace the long-lost poet" (*Paru*, no. 28 [March, 1947], p. 123).

[7] Antonin Artaud, *Pour en finir avec le jugement de Dieu* (Paris: K Editeur, 1948).

[8] This brief sketch, with Vitrac's *The Mysteries of Love* and Robert Aron's *Gigogne*, made up the first program of the Théâtre Alfred Jarry. Artaud described it as a "musical sketch by Antonin Artaud, a lyric work which humoristically denounced the conflict between the cinema and the theater" (*Œuvres*, II, 37–38).

[9] See above, pp. 32–37.

[10] E.g., Weingarten: "Artaud's theater took place in his own life." ("La Force d'un peu plus vivre," in *Cahiers ·de la Compagnie Madeleine Renaud—Jean-Louis Barrault*, p. 149.)

[11] Artaud wrote to Fernand Pouey who had commissioned the broadcast: "I was most pleased by this broadcast, enthused to see that it could provide a miniature model of what I want to do in the Theater of Cruelty." (*Pour en finir*, p. 84.)

[12] Edward Gordon Craig, *On the Art of the Theater* (London: William Heinemann, 1911), p. 22.

[13] *Œuvres*, IV, 187.

[14] Pierre Jean Jouve, "*Les Cenci* d'Antonin Artaud," *La Nouvelle Revue Française*, 23, no. 261 (June, 1935) : 914.

[15] *Œuvres*, II, 83.

[16] *Ibid.*, I, 75.

[17] *Ibid.*, II, 93.

[18] *Ibid.*, V, 26.

[19] In an interview in *Comœdia*, May 6, 1935, Artaud is quoted as saying: "I have borrowed from Stendhal . . . the feel of the period and the color of blood which he has conveyed from an old manuscript. I have borrowed from Shelley all the discipline and lyricism one finds in his work." (*Œuvres*, V, 312.)

[20] *Ibid.*, II, 83.

[21] *Ibid.*, II, 91.

[22] *Ibid.*, IV, 199.

[23] *Ibid.*, II, 83.

[24] Artaud, "Coleridge le traître," *K, Revue de la Poésie*, no. 1–2 (June, 1948), p. 93.

[25] *Œuvres*, II, 91.

[26] *Ibid.*

[27] *Ibid.*, IV, 255–56. This passage is very similar to one from *There Are No Heavens Any More:* "The ruddy light of a forest of torches little by little covers the stage and drinks up all shadow and all other light" (*ibid.*, II, 101).

[28] *Ibid.*, IV, 42.

[29] *Ibid.*, III, 233.

[30] *Ibid.*, II, 91.

[31] *Ibid.*, I, 74–75.

[32] *Ibid.*, II, 86.

[33] *Ibid.*, IV, 244.

[34] *Ibid.*, IV, 407, n. 6.

[35] Pierre Audiat of *Paris Soir*, quoted in *Lettres d'Antonin Artaud à Jean-Louis Barrault*, p. 163.

[36] The most scathing review of *The Cenci* was a saracastic piece by François Porché in the theater column of the *Revue de Paris*. He wrote that no doubt Iya Abdy was "very lovely: with admirable proportions of the figure, with breasts small but well-formed and wide apart like those of the classic Venus, and with a ferocious but sweet mask, a little broad, with the rounded features and blondness of a young lioness, . . . but the stage requires other gifts. Mme Iya Abdy could have had a brilliant career in earlier days—in silent movies" ("Le Théâtre," *La Revue de Paris* 42, no. 10 [May, 1935]: 480).

[37] My efforts to obtain firsthand accounts from people who attended or acted in the play—such as Roger Blin, who acted one of the assassins, and whom I repeatedly queried—have been fruitless.

[38] The most sympathetic review—both favorable and understanding—was that by Pierre Jean Jouve in the *Nouvelle Revue Française*, in which the poet wrote: "The mise en scène by Antonin Artaud continuously animates the stage space in a creative manner: here things are constantly at work. The complex lighting, the movements of the individual and the group, the sounds, the music, all reveal to the spectator that space and time form an affective reality. The union of Artaud's will with that of Balthus is found throughout: the most striking examples of that union appear in the emphatic and somber acting of Artaud himself and in the incandescent beauty and childlike wild action of Iya Abdy." (Jouve, *"Les Cenci* d'Antonin Artaud," p. 914.)

[39] In *Pour en finir*, p. 59.

[40] *Ibid.*, p. 67.

[41] *Ibid.*, p. 20.

[42] *Ibid.*, p. 21.

[43] *Ibid.*, p. 62.

[44] *Ibid.*, p. 69.

[45] *Œuvres*, II, 100–101.

[46] *Ibid.*, IV, 263.

[47] A decade before *The Cenci* Artaud wrote in his first play, *The Spurt of Blood*, the following stage direction: "A silence. One hears a sound like that of a huge wheel which turns and churns up wind" (*Œuvres*, I, 75).

[48] *Œuvres*, IV, 42.

[49] *Ibid.*, IV, 263. A variant reads: "from a different corner of the theater" (IV, 412, n. 2).

[50] Pierre Audiat, quoted in *Lettres d'Antonin Artaud à Jean-Louis Barrault*, p. 164.

[51] *Grand Larousse encyclopédique* (Paris: Larousse, 1963), VII, 129.

[52] Quoted in *Lettres d'Antonin Artaud à Jean-Louis Barrault*, p. 166. Not all critics were so charitable. François Porché wrote: "In that strange *décor*, . . . under those brusque, abbreviated, vulgar lighting effects, in the midst of those snorings, flappings, and whistlings which Roger Désormière labels 'music,' in the midst of those cries of an unbridled amateur uttered by Mr. Artaud, and under the windy gusts of the Russian accent of the leading lady, oh Shelley, what was left of you?" ("Le Théâtre," *La Revue de Paris*, p. 480).

[53] *Œuvres*, IV, 43.

[54] *Ibid.*, IV, 69.

[55] *Ibid.*, II, 92.

[56] *Ibid.*, II, 93–94.

[57] *Ibid.*, I, 79.

[58] *Ibid.*, IV, 245.

[59] Quoted in *Lettres d'Antonin Artaud à Jean-Louis Barrault*, p. 162.

[60] *Œuvres*, II, 88.

[61] Several things in *The Spurt of Blood* besides the surrealist comic opera atmosphere make it possible that this little play is either an imitation or a pastiche of Apollinaire's *Breasts of Tiresias*. The knight in the play runs after the wet nurse asking her to show him her enormous breasts; at the end of the play her breasts have suddenly disappeared. The stage directions at the end of the play seem to provide a clue, an oblique reference to Apollinaire: "The young man and the madame run off like trepaned people." (*Œuvres*, I, 81.)

[62] The play is schematic by design. *The Conquest of Mexico* predates *The Cenci* but is actually closer to Artaud's antitext idea of developing a play right on the stage, as may be seen from an invitation he drafted for the Deharme evening at which he read *Richard II:* "The reading will be accompanied by an original sound track on records / and will be followed by / the first presentation of a new theater scenario / *The Conquest of Mexico* / written with an eye to production directly on the stage." (*Œuvres*, V, 369.)

[63] *Œuvres*, V, 303.

[64] Jouve, *"Les Cenci* d'Antonin Artaud," p. 914.

[65] See the photograph facing page 32 in *K, Revue de la Poésie,* no. 1–2 (June, 1948).

[66] Interview with Pierre Barletier, "A propos de *Cenci,* M. Antonin Artaud nous dit pourquoi il veut écrire un *théâtre de la cruauté,"* in *Œuvres,* V, 309.

[67] *Œuvres,* V, 21.

[68] *Ibid.,* V, 23.

[69] An example of objectification in Ionesco's work is the corpse in *Amedeus* (*Amédée*); of proliferation, the chairs in *The Chairs* (*Les Chaises*). These are hardly inventions, however, and a pertinent example from the beginning of this century is the symbolic mummy in Strindberg's *The Ghost Sonata.*

[70] *Œuvres,* V, 26.

[71] *Ibid.,* V, 27–28.

[72] *Ibid.,* V, 25.

[73] Jouve, *"Les Cenci* d'Antonin Artaud," p. 914.

[74] *Œuvres,* V, 302–3.

[75] *Ibid.,* IV, 95.

[76] Lionel Abel, *Metatheatre: A New View of Dramatic Form* (New York: Hill and Wang, 1963), p. 36.

[77] *Œuvres,* V, 303.

[78] *Ibid.,* V, 309.

[79] *Ibid.,* V, 48.

[80] Antonin Artaud, *Van Gogh, le suicidé de la société* (Paris: K Editeur, 1947).

[81] *Œuvres,* V, 23.

[82] *Héliogabale,* in *ibid.,* VII, 21.

[83] *Œuvres,* VII, 116.

[84] *Ibid.,* VII, 72.

[85] *Ibid.,* IV, 95.

151

# BIBLIOGRAPHY

At the end of this bibliography is a list of works by Artaud which have appeared in English translation.

Abel, Lionel. *Metatheatre: A New View of Dramatic Form.* New York: Hill and Wang, 1963.

Abichard, Robert. "Sous le signe d'Artaud," *La Nouvelle Revue Française* 15, no. 169 (January, 1967) : 108–13.

Adamov, Arthur. "Introduction à Antonin Artaud," *Paru,* no. 29 (April, 1947), pp. 7–12.

———. "L'Œuvre indéfinissable d'Antonin Artaud," *K, Revue de la Poésie,* no. 1–2 (June, 1948), pp. 8–10.

———. "Parce que je l'ai beaucoup aimé . . . ," *Cahiers de la Compagnie Madeleine Renaud—Jean-Louis Barrault,* no. 22–23 (May, 1958), pp. 128–29.

———. [*"Témoignage"*], *84,* no. 5–6 (1948), pp. 138–40.

Agamben, Giorgio. "La 121ª Giornata di Sodoma e Gomorra," *Tempo Presente* 11, no. 3–4 (March–April, 1966) : 58–70.

Albérès, R.-M. *L'Aventure intellectuelle du XXᵉ siècle, panorama des littératures européennes: 1900–1959.* Rev. ed. Paris: Albin Michel, 1959.

"L'Alchimiste." "Antonin Artaud ou l'invitation à la folie," *K, Revue de la Poésie,* no. 1–2 (June, 1948), pp. 79–90.

Allen, Louis. "Antonin Artaud: Cruelty and Reality," *Durham University Journal* 58, no. 1 (December, 1965) : 40–42.

A.M. "Points de repère," *Théâtre Populaire,* no. 18 (May, 1956), pp. 4–8.

*Anthologie de la poésie française depuis le surréalisme.* Edited by M. Béalu. Paris: Editions de Beaune, 1952.

*An Anthology of German Expressionist Drama: A Prelude to the Absurd.* Edited by W. H. Sokel. Garden City, N.Y.: Doubleday, 1963.

Apollinaire, Guillaume. *L'Esprit nouveau et les poëtes.* Paris: Jacques Haumont, 1946.

Aristotle. *The Poetics of Aristotle*. Edited and translated by S. H. Butcher. 3d ed. London: Macmillan, 1902.

Armand-Laroche, J.-L. *Artaud et son double*. Périgueux: Pierre Fanlac, 1964.

Arnold, Paul. "The Artaud Experiment," *Tulane Drama Review* 8, no. 2 (Winter, 1963) : 15–29.

"Artaud for Artaud's Sake," *Encore* 11 (May–June, 1964) : 20–31. (Discussion with Peter Brook and others.)

Artaud, Antonin. "A Alfredo Gangotena," *La Nouvelle Revue Française* 13, no. 149 (May, 1965) : 941–42.

————. *Artaud le momo*. Paris: Bordas, 1947.

————. "Automate personnel," *France–Asie*, no. 30 (September, 1948), pp. 1043–46.

————. "Chiote à l'esprit," *Tel Quel*, no. 2 (Summer, 1960), pp. 3–8.

————. *Ci-gît précédé de la culture indienne*. Paris: K Editeur, 1947.

————. "Coleridge le traître," *K, Revue de la Poésie*, no. 1–2 (June, 1948), pp. 91–97.

————. "La Conquête du Mexique," *La Nef*, no. 63–64 (March–April, 1950), pp. 159–65. (Special double issue entitled "Almanach surréaliste du demi-siécle.")

————. "Les Dix-huit Secondes, La Pierre philosophale, Le Théâtre de séraphin, Là où j'en suis, précédé de visites à Antonin Artaud par Jacques Brenner et Claude Nerguy," *Les Cahiers de la Pléiade* (Spring, 1949), pp. 109–39.

[————]. "D'un voyage au pays des Tarahumaras," *La Nouvelle Revue Française* 25, no. 287 (August, 1937): 232–47. (Published anonymously.)

————. *D'un voyage au pays des Tarahumaras*. Collection "L'Age d'Or." Paris: Fontaine, 1945.

————. "Extrait d'une interview accordée par Antonin Artaud en 1929," *K, Revue de la Poésie*, no. 1–2 (June, 1948), pp. 59–61.

————. ["Extraits de *Suppôts et suppliciations* à paraître chez K Editeur"], *La Nef*, no. 71–72 (December, 1950–January,

1951), pp. 20–23. (Special number, edited by G. Charbonnier, entitled "Humour poétique, 50 inédits.")

———. ["Extraits de *Suppôts et suppliciations* à paraître chez K Editeur"], *Les Temps Modernes* 4, no. 4 (February, 1949): 217–29. (These are not the same pieces as in the previous item.)

———. "Five Open Letters," edited and translated by S. W. Taylor, *Encore* 11 (September–October, 1964): 6–11.

———. *Galapagos, les îles au bout du monde.* Collection "Ecrits et Gravures." Paris: Louis Broder, 1955.

———. *Héliogabale, ou l'anarchiste couronné.* Paris: Denoël et Steele, 1934.

———. "Histoire entre la groume et Dieu," *Fontaine,* no. 57 (December, 1946–January, 1947), pp. 673–77.

———. "L'Intempestive mort et 'L'Aveu' d'Arthur Adamov," *Les Cahiers de la Pléiade* (April, 1947), pp. 138–40.

[———]. "Lettre à Adrienne Monnier," *K, Revue de la Poésie,* no. 1–2 (June, 1948), pp. 114–18.

———. *Lettre contre la Cabbale adressée à Jacques Prevel.* Paris: Jacques Haumont, 1949.

———. "Lettres," *Botteghe Oscure,* no. 8 (1951), pp. 17–30.

———. "Lettres à Maurice Saillet," *K, Revue de la Poésie,* no. 1–2 (June, 1948), pp. 108–14.

———. *Lettres d'Antonin Artaud à Jean-Louis Barrault.* Paris: Bordas, 1952.

———. "Lettres d'Antonin Artaud à Roger Vitrac," edited by H. Béhar, *La Nouvelle Revue Française* 12, no. 136 (April, 1964): 765–76.

———. *Lettres de Rodez.* Paris: GLM, 1948.

———. "Madame Paule Thévenin," *84,* no. 5–6 (1948), pp. 104–6. (A letter to P. Thévenin.)

———. *México,* edited by L. Cardoza y Aragón. Mexico City: Universidad Nacional Autónoma de México, 1962.

———. "Une Note sur la peinture surréaliste en générale, des commentaires de mes dessins," *Tel Quel,* no. 15 (Autumn, 1963), pp. 75–78.

155

Artaud, Antonin. *Œuvres complètes.* (Vols. I, II, III, IV, V, VI, VII
———; 1956 ———) Paris: Gallimard, I (1956), II–III (1961),
IV–V (1964), VI (1966), VII (1967).

———. "Onze Lettres à Anaïs Nin," *Tel Quel,* no. 20 (Winter,
1965), pp. 3–11.

———. *Portraits et dessins.* Paris: Galerie Pierre, 1947.

———. *Pour en finir avec le jugement de Dieu.* Paris: K Editeur,
1948.

———. *Révolte contre la poésie.* Paris, 1944. (The text is by
Artaud, but according to P. Thévenin publication was pre-
dated.)

———. *Supplément aux lettres de Rodez, suivi de Coleridge le
traître.* Paris: GLM, 1949.

———. "Sur les chimères," *Tel Quel,* no. 22 (Summer, 1965), pp.
3–13.

———. *Les Tarahumaras.* Décines, Isère: L'Arbalète, 1955.

———. "Le Théâtre de la cruauté," *84,* no. 5–6 (1948), pp.
121–30.

———. "Le Théâtre et la science," *Théâtre Populaire,* no. 5
(January–February, 1954), pp. 5–9. (A note states that the text
first appeared in *L'Arbalète,* no. 13 [Summer, 1948].)

———. *Le Théâtre et son double.* "Collection Métamorphoses."
Paris: Gallimard, 1938; reprinted, 1944; re-edited in *Œuvres
complétes,* Vol. IV (1964); re-edited in "Collection Idées,"
1966.

———. "Trois Lettres inédites d'Antonin Artaud au Docteur
Ferdière," *La Tour de Feu,* no. 63–64 (December, 1959), pp.
6–15.

———. *Van Gogh, le suicidé de la société.* Paris: K Editeur,
1947.

———. *Vie et mort de Satan le feu, suivi de textes mexicains pour
un nouveau mythe.* Edited by S. Berna. Paris: Arcanes, 1953.

*Aspects of Drama and the Theatre.* Sydney: Sydney University
Press, 1965. (A symposium including R. L. Chambers, "Antonin Artaud and the Contemporary French Theater," pp.
113–42.)

156

Audiberti, [Jacques]. "Le Salut par la peau," *K, Revue de la Poésie*, no. 1–2 (June, 1948), pp. 62–64.

Barrault, Jean-Louis. "L'Acteur: 'athlète affectif,'" *Cahiers de la Compagnie Madeleine Renaud—Jean-Louis Barrault*, no. 29 (February, 1960), pp. 86–95.

———. *Nouvelles Réflexions sur le théâtre.* "Bibliothèque d'Esthétique." Paris: Flammarion, 1959.

———. "Un Personnage de feu . . . ," *Arts* (February 26–March 4, 1958), p. 3.

———. *Le Phénomène théâtral.* "Zaharoff Lecture for 1961—Oxford." Oxford: Clarendon Press, 1961.

———. *Réflexions sur le théâtre.* Paris: Jacques Vautrain, 1949.

Bataille, Marcel. "La Dernière Conférence," *France–Asie*, no. 30 (September, 1948), pp. 1047–48.

Béalu, Marcel. "Quand tout le monde joue," *La Tour de Feu*, no. 63–64 (December, 1959), p. 104.

Beck, Julian. "Thoughts on the Theater from Jail," *New York Times*, February 21, 1965, sec. 2, p. 3.

Beigbeder, Marc. *Le Théâtre en France depuis la libération.* Paris: Bordas, 1959.

Benay, J., and Kuhn, R. *Le Théâtre de la cruauté. Panorama du théâtre nouveau*, Vol. II. New York: Appleton-Century-Crofts, 1967.

Benmussa, Simone. "Antonin Artaud et la bataille des cormorans," *Cahiers de la Compagnie Madeleine Renaud—Jean-Louis Barrault*, no. 29 (February, 1960), pp. 118–21.

Bentley, Eric. *In Search of Theater.* New York: Vintage Books, 1959.

Berger, Pierre. "Artaud, notre étranger . . . ," *Carrefour*, July 8, 1959, p. 21.

Bertelé, René. *"Le Théâtre et son double* ou le chant d'un hérétique," *Mercure de France* 352, no. 1213 (November, 1964): 508–14.

Bisiaux, Marcel. ["Témoignage"], *84*, no. 5–6 (1948), pp. 141–43.

Blanchot, Maurice. "Artaud," *La Nouvelle Revue Française* 4, no. 47 (November, 1956): 873–81.

Blanchot, Maurice. "La Cruelle Raison poétique," *Cahiers de la Compagnie Madeleine Renaud—Jean-Louis Barrault,* no. 22–23 (May, 1958), pp. 66–73.

———. *Le Livre à venir.* 2d ed. Paris: Gallimard, 1959.

Boll, André. *La Mise en scène contemporaine, son évolution.* Collection "Choses et Gens du Théâtre." Paris: Editions de la Nouvelle Revue Critique, 1944.

Bonneton, André. *Le Naufrage prophétique d'Antonin Artaud.* Paris: Henri Lefebvre, 1961.

*The Book of the Dead: The Hieroglyphic Transcript of the Papyrus of ANI.* Edited and translated by E. A. W. Budge. New Hyde Park, N.Y.: University Books, 1960.

Boschère, Jean de. "Une Âme trop vaste (à propos d'Antonin Artaud)," *Cahiers du Sud* 39, no. 316 (1952) : 420–25.

———. ["Extraits de *Journal d'un rebelle solitaire*"], *France-Asie,* no. 30 (September, 1948), pp. 1029–33.

Bosquet, Alain. "Antonin Artaud ou la vocation du délire," *La Revue de Paris* 66 (March, 1959) : 96–104.

Bouloc, Denys-Paul. "Antonin Artaud à Rodez," *La Tour de Feu,* no. 63–64 (December, 1959), pp. 72–74.

Bounoure et Caradec, Gaston. "Antonin Artaud et le cinéma," *K, Revue de la Poésie,* no. 1–2 (June, 1948), pp. 49–61.

Bowers, Faubion. *Theatre in the East: A Survey of Asian Dance and Drama.* New York and London: Grove Press and Evergreen Books, 1956.

Brasillach, Robert. *Animateurs du théâtre.* Paris: La Table Ronde, 1954.

Brasseur de Bourbourg, L'Abbé. *Popol-Vuh, le Livre Sacré et les mythes de l'antiquité américaine.* Paris: Auguste Durand, 1861.

Breitman, Michel. "Les Héritiers abusifs doivent cesser de nuire," *Arts* (February 25–March 4, 1958), pp. 1, 4.

Brenner, Jacques. "Antonin Artaud," *Les Cahiers de la Pléiade* (Spring, 1949), pp. 109–10.

Bresson, Henri-Cartier. *Les Danses à Bali.* "Collection 'Huit.'" Paris: Robert Delpire, 1954. (The preface is a reprinting of the NRF version of Artaud's "Le Théâtre balinais.")

158

Breton, André. "André Breton parle d'Artaud pour *La Tour de Feu*," *La Tour de Feu*, no. 63–64 (December, 1959), pp. 3–5.

———. *La Clé des champs*. Paris: Editions du Sagittaire, 1953.

———. *Entretiens, 1913–1952*. 10th ed. Paris: Gallimard, 1952.

———. *Manifestes du surréalisme*. Paris: J.-J. Pauvert, 1962.

———. *Les Pas Perdus*. 8th ed. Paris: Gallimard, 1924.

Brook, Peter, *et al.* "Marat / Sade Forum," *Tulane Drama Review* 10, no. 4 (Summer, 1966) : 214–37.

Brustein, Robert. *The Theatre of Revolt*. Boston and Toronto: Atlantic–Little, Brown, 1964.

Bryen, Camille. "Antonin Artaud," *France–Asie*, no. 30 (September, 1948), pp. 1037–40.

Büchner, Georg. *The Plays of Georg Büchner*. Edited and translated by G. Dunlop. New York: Irving Ravin, 1952.

Burucoa, Christiane. "Antonin Artaud ou la 'difficulté d'être,' " *Entretiens*, no. 9 (Spring, 1957), pp. 19–25.

*Cahiers de la Compagnie Madeleine Renaud—Jean-Louis Barrault*, no. 22–23 (May, 1958). (Special double homage issue entitled "Antonin Artaud et le théâtre de notre temps.")

Camus, Albert. *L'Homme révolté*. "Collection Idées." Paris: Gallimard, 1951.

———. *Méditation sur le théâtre et la vie*. Liège: Editions Dynamo, 1961.

———. *Le Mythe de Sisyphe*. "Collection Idées." Paris: Gallimard, 1942.

Cano de Castro, Manuel. "Rencontre d'Artaud avec les tarots," *K, Revue de la Poésie*, no. 1–2 (June, 1948), pp. 119–23.

Capin, Jean. "Bibliographie des écrits sur Antonin Artaud," *Cahiers de la Compagnie Madeleine Renaud—Jean-Louis Barrault*, no. 22–23 (May, 1958), pp. 216–19.

Chabert, Pierre. "Artaud en tête," *La Tour de Feu*, no. 63–64 (December, 1959), pp. 88–103.

Chaleix, Pierre. "Avant le surréalisme, Artaud chez le Dr Toulouse," *La Tour de Feu*, no. 63–64 (December, 1959), pp. 55–60. (Interview with Mme Toulouse.)

Chambers, Ross. " 'La Magie du Réel': Antonin Artaud and the

Experience of the Theatre," *Australian Journal of French Studies* 3, no. 1 (January–April, 1966) : 51–65.

Charbonnier, Georges. *Antonin Artaud.* Collection "Poètes d'Aujourd'hui." Paris: Pierre Seghers, 1959.

Chiaromonte, Nicola. "Artaud e la sua doppia idea del teatro," *Tempo Presente* 11, no. 3–4 (March–April, 1966), pp. 48–58.

Clancier, Georges-Emmanuel. *De Rimbaud au surréalisme, panorama critique.* Paris: Pierre Seghers, 1955.

*Codex Nuttall: Facsimile of an Ancient Mexican Codex Belonging to Lord Zouche of Harynworth, England.* Introduction by Z. Nuttall. Cambridge, Mass.: Peabody Museum, 1902.

"Les Conférences," *Paru,* no. 28 (March, 1947), p. 123.

"Conversation avec André Masson, propos recueillis par S. B. et J. C.," *Cahiers de la Compagnie Madeleine Renaud—Jean-Louis Barrault,* no. 22–23 (May, 1958), pp. 11–15.

Cor, Lawrence W. "French Views on Language in the Theater," *French Review* 35 (October, 1961) : 11–18.

Corrigan, Robert W. "The Theatre in Search of a Fix," *Tulane Drama Review* 5, no. 4 (June, 1961) : 21–35.

Cortázar, Julio. "Muerte de Antonin Artaud," *Sur* 16 (May, 1948) : 80–82. (Followed by "Una Carta de Antonin Artaud" [a translation of the September 17, 1945, letter from Rodez], pp. 82–85.)

Corti, Victor. "Introduction [to Artaud's 'To End God's Judgment']," *Tulane Drama Review* 9, no. 3 (Spring, 1965) : 56–59.

Craig, Edward Gordon. *On the Art of the Theatre.* London: William Heinemann, 1911.

Cuny, Alain. "Artaud de son vivant," *K, Revue de la Poésie,* no. 1–2 (June, 1948), pp. 25–28.

———. ["Témoignage"], *84,* no. 5–6 (1948), pp. 145–46.

Danzel, Theodor-Wilhelm. "The Psychology of Ancient Mexican Symbolism." In *Spiritual Disciplines: Papers from the Eranos Yearbooks.* Bollingen Series XXX, vol. 4. New York: Pantheon Books, 1960, pp. 102–14.

Decaunes, Luc. "A propos d'un nouveau messie," *Cahiers du Sud* 35, no. 291 (1948) : 365–69.

Delanglade, Frédéric. "Antonin Artaud chez Gaston Ferdière," *La Tour de Feu,* no. 63–64 (December, 1959), pp. 75–78.

Derrida, Jacques. "La Parole soufflée," *Tel Quel,* no. 20 (Winter, 1965), pp. 41–67.

———. "Le Théâtre de la cruauté et la clôture de la représentation," *Critique* 22, no. 230 (July, 1966) : 595–618.

Desnos, Youki. *Les Confidences de Youki.* Paris: Arthème Fayard, 1957.

Desternes, Jean. "Ci-gît Antonin Artaud," *La Table Ronde* (April, 1948), pp. 692–98.

Diderot, Denis. *Œuvres esthétiques.* Edited by P. Vermière. Paris: Garnier Frères, 1959.

Dullin, Charles. "Lettre à Roger Blin," *K, Revue de la Poésie,* no. 1–2 (June, 1948), pp. 21–24.

Ebin, D., ed. *The Drug Experience.* New York: Orion Press, 1961.

Eliade, Mircea. *Aspects du mythe.* "Collection Idées." Paris: Gallimard, 1963.

*Encyclopédie du théâtre contemporain.* Edited by G. Quéant with the collaboration of F. Towarnicki. Collection "Théâtre de France." 2 vols. Paris: Olivier Perrin, 1957–59.

Ernst, Earle. *The Kabuki Theatre.* New York: Grove Press, 1956.

Esslin, Martin. "The Theater of Cruelty," *New York Times Magazine,* March 4, 1966, pp. 22–23, 71–74.

———. "The Theatre of the Absurd," *Tulane Drama Review* 4, no. 4 (May, 1960) : 3–15.

———. *The Theatre of the Absurd.* Garden City, N.Y. Doubleday, 1961.

———. "Violence," *Encore* 11 (May–June, 1964) : 6–15.

Faye, Jean Pierre. "Artaud vu par Blin," *Les Lettres Françaises,* January 21, 1965, pp. 1, 5.

Ferdière, Gaston. "J'ai soigné Antonin Artaud," *La Tour de Feu,* no. 63–64 (December, 1959), pp. 28–37.

Fergusson, Francis. *The Idea of a Theater.* Garden City, N.Y.: Doubleday, 1953.

Fernandez, James W. "Principles of Opposition and Vitality in

Fang Aesthetics," *Journal of Aesthetics and Art Criticism* 25, no. 1 (Fall, 1966) : 53–64.

Follain, Jean. "Sur Artaud," *La Tour de Feu*, no. 63–64 (December, 1959), pp. 70–71.

Ford, John. *Five Plays*. Edited by H. Ellis. 2d printing. New York: Hill and Wang, 1960.

Fowlie, Wallace. *Dionysus in Paris: A Guide to Contemporary French Theater*. New York: Meridian Books, 1960.

―――. "The New French Theater: Artaud, Beckett, Genet, Ionesco," *Sewanee Review* 67 (1959) : 643–57.

Frank, André. "Antonin Artaud," *La Revue Théâtrale* 5, no. 13 (Summer, 1950) : 26–37.

―――. "Artaud et le Théâtre de la Cruauté," *Encyclopédie du théâtre contemporain*. Paris: Olivier Perrin, 1959. 2:54–55.

―――. "D'Antonin Artaud aux cérémonies hittites," *Cahiers de la Compagnie Madeleine Renaud—Jean-Louis Barrault*, no. 31 (November, 1960), pp. 108–11. (Special issue entitled "Théâtres lointains.")

―――. "De la prise à la gorge à la prise à témoin . . . ," *Cahiers de la Compagnie Madeleine Renaud—Jean-Louis Barrault*, no. 22–23 (May, 1958), pp. 211–15.

―――. "Il a voulu réinstaller la magie sur la scène," *Arts* (February 26–March 4, 1958), p. 3.

Fraser, James George. *The Golden Bough: A Study in Magic and Religion*. Abridged edition in one volume. New York: Macmillan, 1923.

Freud, Sigmund. *Character and Culture*. Edited by P. Rieff. New York: Collier Books, 1963.

―――. *Totem and Taboo*. 2d ed. New York: Random House, 1961.

Friedländer, Max J. *Die Altniederländische Malerei*. Vol. 10. Leiden: Sijthoffs Uitgevermij, 1934.

―――. *Lucas van Leyden*. Berlin: Walter de Gruyter, 1963.

Gance, Abel. "Par delà la mort," *Cahiers de la Compagnie Madeleine Renaud—Jean-Louis Barrault*, no. 22–23 (May, 1958), pp. 74–75.

162

Gheerbrant, Bernard. "Bibliographie des ouvrages en langue française de Antonin Artaud," *K, Revue de la Poésie,* no. 1–2 (June, 1948), pp. 132–37.

Gide, André. "Extrait d'une lettre d'André Gide à Henri Thomas, communiqué par Pierre Loeb," *Cahiers de la Compagnie Madeleine Renaud—Jean-Louis Barrault,* no. 22–23 (May, 1958), pp. 126–27.

————. ["Témoignage"], *84,* no. 5–6 (1948), pp. 150–51; reprinted as "Antonin Artaud" in *Eloges* (Neuchâtel and Paris: Ides et Calendes, 1948), pp. 143–46; and in *Feuillets d'automne, précédés de quelques récents écrits* (Paris: Mercure de France, 1949), pp. 132–34.

Ginestier, Paul. *Le Théâtre contemporian dans le monde, essai de critique esthétique.* Paris: Presses Universitaires de France, 1961.

Glantz, Margo. "Antonin Artaud: la crueldad y el absurdo," *Revista de Bellas Artes,* no. 1 (January–February, 1965), pp. 72–75.

Goll, Yvan. "Manifeste du surréalisme," *Surréalisme,* no. 1 (October, 1924), no pagination.

————. *Mathusalem: oder der ewige Bürger.* Potsdam: Gustav Kiepenheuer, 1922.

Goodman, Paul. "Obsessed by Theater," *Nation,* November 29, 1958, pp. 412–14.

Gorelik, Mordecai. *New Theatres for Old.* New York: E. P. Dutton, 1962.

Gourmont, Rémy de. "Théâtre muet." In *Œuvres de Rémy de Gourmont.* Paris: Mercure de France, 1932. 6:213–21.

Gray, Paul. "The Theatre of the Marvelous," *Tulane Drama Review* 7, no. 4 (Summer, 1963): 133–60.

Gresset, Michel. "Création et cruauté chez Beckett," *Tel Quel,* no. 15 (Autumn, 1963), pp. 58–65.

Grisson, Pierre. "Artaud et son double," *France–Asie* 9 (1953): 1043–45.

Gross, John. "Amazing Reductions," *Encounter* 23 (September, 1964): 50–52.

Gross, John. "Darkness Risible," *Encounter* 23 (October, 1964): 41–43.

———. "1793 & All That," *Encounter* 23 (November, 1964): 58–60.

Grossvogel, David I. *Four Playwrights and a Postscript: Brecht, Ionesco, Beckett, Genet.* Ithaca, N.Y.: Cornell University Press, 1962.

———. *20th Century French Drama.* New York and London: Columbia University Press, 1961. (Originally published under the title *The Self-Conscious Stage in Modern French Drama.*)

Guicharnaud, Jacques. *Modern French Theatre from Giraudoux to Beckett.* New Haven: Yale University Press, 1961.

Gullón, Ricardo. "El Caso Artaud," *Insula* 4, no. 47 (November 15, 1949): 3.

Hahn, Otto. "Portrait d'Antonin Artaud," *Les Temps Modernes* 17, no. 192 (May, 1962): 1592–1619; no. 193 (June, 1962): 1854–82.

Hauger, George. "When Is a Play Not a Play," *Tulane Drama Review* 5, no. 2 (December, 1960): 54–64.

Hegel. *On Tragedy.* Edited by A. and H. Paolucci. Garden City, N.Y.: Doubleday, 1962.

Hellman, Helen. "Hallucination and Cruelty in Artaud and Ghelderode," *French Review* 41, no. 1 (October, 1967): 1–10.

Hivnor, Mary Otis. "Barrault and Artaud," *Partisan Review* 15 (March, 1948): 332–38.

"Holland Salvages Relics," *New York Times,* June 30, 1931, p. 8.

Hort, Jean. *Antonin Artaud, le suicidé de la société.* Geneva: Editions Connaître, 1960.

———. *Les Théâtres du Cartel et leurs animateurs: Pitoëff, Baty, Jouvet, Dullin.* Geneva: Skira, 1944.

Humeau, Edmond. "La Santé de la poésie," *La Tour de Feu,* no. 63–64 (December, 1959), pp. 138–44.

Ionesco, Eugène. "Ni un dieu, ni un démon," *Cahiers de la Compagnie Madeleine Renaud—Jean-Louis Barrault,* no. 22–23 (May, 1958), pp. 130–34.

Ionesco, Eugène. *Notes et contre-notes.* Collection "Pratique du Théâtre." Paris: Gallimard, 1962.

———. "The Writer and His Problems," *Encounter* 23 (September, 1964): 3–15.

Jarry, Alfred. *Tout Ubu.* Edited by M. Saillet. Paris: Le Livre de Poche, 1962.

Jouffroy, Alain. "Pour un théâtre de la cruauté," *L'Express,* July 30, 1964, pp. 29–30.

Jouve, Pierre Jean. *"Les Cenci d'Antonin Artaud,"* *La Nouvelle Revue Française* 23, no. 261 (June, 1935): 910–15.

Jung, C. G. *Psyche and Symbol: A Selection from the Writings of C. G. Jung.* Edited by V. S. de Laszlo. Garden City, N.Y.: Doubleday, 1958.

*K, Revue de la Poésie,* no. 1–2 (June, 1948). (Special double homage issue entitled "Antonin Artaud, textes, témoignages, documents.")

Keats, John, and Shelley, Percy Bysshe. *Complete Poetical Works.* New York: Modern Library, n.d.

Keene, Donald. *Japanese Literature.* New York: Grove Press, 1955.

Klée, Paul. "Eléments pour une esthétique," *Les Temps Modernes* 18, no. 200 (January, 1963): 1204–15.

Knapp, Bettina. "An Interview with Roger Blin," *Tulane Drama Review* 7, no. 3 (Spring, 1963): 111–24.

———. "Artaud: A New Type of Magic," *Yale French Studies,* no. 31 (May, 1964), pp. 87–98.

Koch, Stephen. "On Artaud," *Tri-Quarterly,* no. 6 (1966), pp. 29–37.

Kubie, Lawrence S. *Neurotic Distortion of the Creative Process.* New York: Noonday Press, 1961.

Kustow, Michael. "Sur les traces d'Artaud," *Esprit* 33, no. 338 (May, 1965): 958–63.

Kyrou, Ado. *Le Surréalisme au cinéma.* Paris: Arcanes, 1953.

Lao Tzu. *Tao Teh Ching.* Edited by P. K. T. Sih; translated by J. C. H. Wu. New York: St. John's University Press, 1961.

Lautréamont. *Œuvres complètes.* Paris: Corti, 1953.

Lebesque, Morvan. "Le Théâtre aux enfers: Artaud, Beckett et quelques autres," *Cahiers de la Compagnie Madeleine Renaud—Jean-Louis Barrault,* no. 22–23 (May, 1958), pp. 191–96.

Leminier, Georges. "From Stage Design to the Organization of Scenic Space," *World Theatre* 10 (Autumn, 1961): 251–61.

Lièvre, Pierre. "Théâtre," *Mercure de France* 46, no. 889 (July, 1935): 142–46.

Lindsjö, Inga. "Kung Ubu, Dockteatern, och Absurdismen," *Ord och Bild* 75, no. 1 (1965): 52–60.

Loeb, Edouard. "Antonin Artaud," *Arts* (March 12, 1948), p. 2.

———. "Antonin Artaud," *K, Revue de la Poésie,* no. 1–2 (June, 1948), pp. 71–73.

Loeb, Pierre. "Dessinateur et critique," *Cahiers de la Compagnie Madeleine Renaud—Jean-Louis Barrault,* no. 22–23 (May, 1958), pp. 115–18.

Maeterlinck, Maurice. *Douze Chansons.* Collection "Les Contemporains." Paris: Stock, 1923.

———. *Pelléas et Mélisande.* In *Théâtre.* 31st ed. Brussels: Paul Lacomblez, 1912. 2:1–113.

Malaussena, Marie-Ange. "Affaire Antonin Artaud: ce qu'il faut savoir," *La Tour de Feu,* no. 63–64 (December, 1959), pp. 38–54.

———. "Antonin Artaud," *La Revue Théâtrale* 8, no. 23 (1953): 39–57.

———. "Notes bio-bibliographiques," *La Tour de Feu,* no. 63–64 (December, 1959), pp. 79–82.

Malraux, André. *La Tentation de l'occident.* Paris: Grasset, 1926.

Maritain, Jacques. *Creative Intuition in Art and Poetry.* New York: Meridian Books, 1955.

Marowitz, Charles. "Letter from London," *Nation,* September 7, 1964, pp. 99–100.

———. "Notes on the Theatre of Cruelty," *Tulane Drama Review* 11, no. 2 (Winter, 1966): 152–72.

"Martenot," *Grand Larousse encyclopédique* (Paris: Larousse, 1963). 7:129–30.

Masson, André. "Artaud, lui-même," *Cahiers de la Compagnie Madeleine Renaud—Jean-Louis Barrault*, no. 22–23 (May, 1958), pp. 9–10.

Mauriac, Claude. *L'Alittérature contemporaine.* Paris: Albin Michel, 1958.

Ménard, René. "Antonin Artaud et la condition poétique," *Critique* 11, no. 119 (April, 1957): 299–310.

Milne, Tom. "Cruelty, Cruelty," *Encore* 11 (March–April, 1964): 9–12.

———. "Reflections on *The Screens*," *Encore* 11 (July–August, 1964): 21–25.

Muller, André. "Techniques de l'avant-garde," *Théâtre Populaire*, no. 18 (May, 1956), pp. 21–29.

Nadeau, Maurice. "La Danse à l'endroit," *K, Revue de la Poésie*, no. 1–2 (June, 1948), pp. 98–100.

———. *Histoire du surréalisme.* Collection "Pierres Vives." Paris: Editions du Seuil, 1945.

———. *Littérature présente.* Paris: Corrêa, 1952.

Nerguy, Claude. "Antonin Artaud, quelques jours avant sa mort," *Les Cahiers de la Pléiade* (Spring, 1949), pp. 111–12.

Niccolini, G.-B. *Opere.* 2 vols. Florence: Le Monnier, 1844.

Nin, Anaïs. *The Diary of Anaïs Nin, 1931–1934.* Edited by G. Stuhlmann. New York: Swallow Press, 1966.

———. *The Diary of Anaïs Nin, 1934–1939.* Edited by G. Stuhlmann. New York: Swallow Press, 1967.

Paris, Jean. "The French Avant-Garde Theatre," *American Society Legion of Honor Magazine* 30 (1962): 45–52.

Parisot, Henri. "Ne laissez pas les psychiatres jouer avec la poésie," *K, Revue de la Poésie*, no. 1–2 (June, 1948), pp. 74–78.

Patri, Aimé. "Antonin Artaud," *France–Asie*, no. 30 (September, 1948), pp. 1033–36.

Pichette, Henri. "Adresse à ceux qui vont bientôt comprendre," *K, Revue de la Poésie*, no. 1–2 (June, 1948), pp. 29–32.

Picon, Gaëtan. *Panorama de la nouvelle littérature française.* 23d ed. rev. Paris: Gallimard, 1949.

———. *L'Usage de la lecture.* 2 vols. Paris: Mercure de France, 1960–61.

*Playwrights on Playwriting.* Edited by T. Cole. 3d printing. New York: Hill and Wang, 1963.

Polieri, Jacques. "Un Spectacle magique," *Cahiers de la Compagnie Madeleine Renaud—Jean-Louis Barrault,* no. 22–23 (May, 1958), pp. 162–65.

Porché François. "Le Théâtre," *La Revue de Paris* 42, no. 10 (May, 1935) : 473–80.

Poulet, Robert. *La Lanterne magique,* Vol. 1. Paris: Debresse, 1956.

Pound, Ezra. *ABC of Reading.* Norfolk, Conn.: New Directions, n.d.

Pronko, Leonard Cabell. *Avant-Garde: The Experimental Theater in France.* Berkeley and Los Angeles: University of California Press, 1962.

———. *Theater East and West: Perspectives toward a Total Theater.* Berkeley and Los Angeles: University of California Press, 1967.

Pucciani, Oreste F. "Tragedy, Genet and *The Maids,*" *Tulane Drama Review* 7, no. 3 (Spring, 1963) : 42–59.

*84,* no. 5–6 (1948). (Special double issue entitled "Antonin Artaud.")

Reeves, Geoffrey. "Camus and the Drama of Assassination," *Encore* 11 (January–February, 1964) : 6–15.

*La Révolution Surréaliste,* no. 1 (December, 1924), no. 2 (January, 1925), no. 3 (April, 1925), no. 4 (July, 1925), no. 5 (October, 1925).

Rivière, Claude. "Il y a dix ans mourait Antonin Artaud," *Réforme,* March 29, 1958, p. 10.

Robert, Marthe. "Je suis cet insurgé du corps . . . ," *Cahiers de la Compagnie Madeleine Renaud—Jean-Louis Barrault,* no. 22–23 (May, 1958), pp. 49–60.

Rousselot, Jean. "Dernière Rencontre avec Antonin Artaud," *France–Asie*, no. 30 (September, 1948), pp. 1040–42.

———. *Panorama critique des nouveaux poètes français*. Paris: Pierre Seghers, 1952.

Royer, Jean-Michel. "Connaissance et reconnaissance," *Cahiers de la Compagnie Madeleine Renaud—Jean-Louis Barrault*, no. 22–23 (May, 1958), pp. 135–48.

Saillet, Maurice. "Antonin Artaud," *Mercure de France* 103, no. 1017 (May, 1948): 102–13.

———. "Tête-à-tête avec Antonin Artaud," *K, Revue de la Poésie*, no. 1–2 (June, 1948), pp. 103–7.

"Saint Artaud," *Times Literary Supplement*, March 18, 1965, p. 214.

Schechner, Richard. "The Inner and the Outer Reality," *Tulane Drama Review* 7, no. 3 (Spring, 1963): 187–217.

"The Screens," *Tulane Drama Review* 11, no. 4 (Summer, 1967): 105–12. (Interviews with Amidou and Roger Blin by B. Knapp and P. Gray.)

Séjourné, Laurette. *Burning Water: Thought and Religion in Ancient Mexico*. New York: Grove Press, 1960.

Seligmann, Kurt. *The Mirror of Magic*. New York: Pantheon, 1948.

Sellin, Eric. "Antonin Artaud and an Objectified Language of the Stage," *L'Esprit Créateur* 6, no. 1 (Spring, 1966): 31–35.

———. "Antonin Artaud and the Oriental Theater." In *Asian Drama: A Collection of Festival Papers*. Edited by H. W. Wells. Vermillion, S. D.: The College of Fine Arts—University of South Dakota, 1966. Pp. 142–48.

———. "The Dramatic Concepts of Antonin Artaud," *Dissertation Abstracts* 26, no. 9 (March, 1966): 5445.

———. "The Oriental Influence in Modern Western Drama," *France–Asie* 21, no. 187 (Autumn, 1966): 85–92.

Seneca. *Thyestes*. Edited by M. Hades. Indianapolis and New York: Bobbs-Merrill, 1957.

Seymour, Alan. "Artaud's Cruelty," *London Magazine* 3, no. 12 (March, 1964): 59–64.

Shattuck, Roger. *The Banquet Years, The Arts in France: 1885–1918.* Garden City, N.Y.: Doubleday, 1961.

Smith, Sir William. *Smaller Classical Dictionary.* New York: E. P. Dutton, 1958.

Sokel, Walter H. *The Writer in Extremis: Expressionism in Twentieth-Century German Literature.* Stanford, Calif.: Stanford University Press, 1959.

Sollers, Philippe. "La Pensée émet des signes," *Tel Quel,* no. 20 (Winter, 1965), pp. 12–24.

Sontag, Susan. "Ionesco: The Theater of the Banal," *New York Review of Books,* July 9, 1964, pp. 9–11.

———. "Marat / Sade / Artaud," *Partisan Review* 32, no. 2 (Spring, 1965) : 210–19.

Soupault, Philippe. "Alfred Jarry," *Cahiers de la Compagnie Madeleine Renaud—Jean-Louis Barrault,* no. 22–23 (May, 1958), pp. 174–81.

———. "Sa Poésie était une façon de fermer les yeux," *Arts* (February 26–March 4), 1958, p. 3.

Stendhal. *Chroniques italiennes.* Edited by H. Martineau. 2 vols. Paris: Le Divan, 1929.

Strindberg, August. *Six Plays of Strindberg.* Edited and translated by E. Sprigge. Garden City, N.Y.: Doubleday, 1955.

Temkine, Raymonde. "Fils naturel d'Artaud," *Les Lettres Nouvelles* (May–June, 1966), pp. 127–37.

Thévenin, Paule. "Antonin Artaud dans la vie," *Tel Quel,* no. 20 (Winter, 1965), pp. 25–40.

———. "Correspondance," *Les Lettres Nouvelles,* no. 41 (September, 1956), pp. 363–67. (A letter to Maurice Nadeau.)

———. "L'Imbécillisation par la 'Beat Generation,' " *Tel Quel,* no. 24 (Winter, 1966), pp. 93–94 .

———. "A Letter on Artaud," *Tulane Drama Review* 9, no. 3 (Spring, 1965) : 99–117. (Translation of "Artaud dans la vie.")

———. "1896–1948," *Cahiers de la Compagnie Madeleine Renaud—Jean-Louis Barrault,* no. 22–23 (May, 1958), pp. 17–45.

Thibaudet, Jean. "Artaud, homme de théâtre," *France-Observateur*, July 16, 1964, p. 14.

Thomas, Henri. "Le Point mort," *Les Cahiers de la Pléiade* (Spring, 1948), pp. 15–17.

——. ["Témoignage"], *84*, no. 5–6 (1948), pp. 140–41.

*La Tour de Feu*, no. 63–64 (December, 1959). (Special double homage issue entitled "Antonin Artaud ou la santé des poètes.")

Tourret, Fernand. "L'Artaud des années mortes," *La Tour de Feu*, no. 63–64 (December, 1959), pp. 61–67.

Tzara, Tristan. "Antonin Artaud, et le désespoir de la connaissance," *Les Lettres Françaises*, March 25, 1948, pp. 1, 2.

Vannier, Jean. "Langage de l'avant-garde," *Théâtre Populaire*, no. 18 (May, 1956), pp. 30–39.

——. "A Theatre of Language," *Tulane Drama Review* 7, no. 3 (Spring, 1963) : 180–86.

Vigée, Claude. "Les Artistes de la faim," *La Table Ronde*, no. 112 (April, 1957), pp. 43–64.

——. "Metamorphoses of Modern Poetry," *Comparative Literature* 7 (Spring, 1955) : 97–120.

Vilar, Jean. *De la tradition théâtrale*. Paris: Gallimard, 1955.

Virmaux, Alain. "Artaud and Film," *Tulane Drama Review* 11, no. 1 (Fall, 1966) : 154–65.

Vitrac, Roger. *Théâtre*, Vol. 1. 6th ed. Paris: Gallimard, 1946.

Wahl, Jean. " 'Antonin Artaud? Personne,' " *Cahiers de la Compagnie Madeleine Renaud—Jean-Louis Barrault*, no. 22–23 (May, 1958), pp. 61–65.

Weingarten, Romain. "La Force d'un peu plus vivre," *Cahiers de la Compagnie Madeleine Renaud—Jean-Louis Barrault*, no. 22–23 (May, 1958), pp. 149–56.

——. "Relire Artaud," *Théâtre Populaire*, no. 18 (May, 1956), pp. 9–20.

Wellwarth, George E. "Antonin Artaud: Prophet of the Avant-Garde Theatre," *Drama Survey* 2 (Winter, 1963) : 276–87.

——. *The Theater of Protest and Paradox: Developments in*

*the Avant-Garde Drama.* New York: New York University Press, 1964.

Wunderlich, Lawrence. "A Playwright's Microcosm," *Chelsea,* no. 16 (1965), pp. 39–62.

Yeats, William Butler. *Essays and Introductions.* New York: Macmillan, 1961.

WORKS BY ARTAUD TRANSLATED INTO ENGLISH

*Antonin Artaud Anthology.* Edited by J. Hirschman. San Francisco: City Lights Books, 1965.

Artaud, Antonin. "Artaud-Rivière Correspondence." Translated by B. Frechtman, *Exodus,* no. 3 (Spring–Summer, 1960), pp. 51–70.

———. "Black Poet." Translated by P. Zweig, *Chelsea,* no. 13 ["Special French Issue"] (June, 1963), p. 21.

———. *Black Poet and Other Texts.* Introduction and translations by P. Zweig. Collection "Passeport." Paris: Lettres modernes, 1966. (The French is presented beside the translations under the title, *Poète noir et autres textes.*

———. "Concerning a Journey to the Land of the Tarahumaras [preceded by a letter to Henri Parisot]." Translated by D. Rattray, *City Lights Journal,* no. 2 (1964), pp. 81–100.

———. "Correspondence with Jacques Rivière," Translated by J. Ashbery," *Art and Literature,* no. 6 (Autumn, 1965), pp. 9–27.

———. "Dinner Is Served," "Letter to the Chancellors of the European University," "Address to the Pope," "Address to the Dalai Lama," and "Letter to the Buddhist Schools," in Patrick Waldberg, *Surrealism* (New York and Toronto: McGraw-Hill, n.d.), pp. 56–60.

———. "Five Open Letters." Edited and translated by S. W. Taylor, *Encore* 11 (September–October, 1964) : 6–11.

———. "From 'The Nerve Scale,'" *Origin: A Quarterly for the Creative,* no. 11 (Autumn, 1953), p. 133.

———. "From *The Theater and Its Double.*" Translated by M. C. Richards, *Origin: A Quarterly for the Creative,* no. 11 (Autumn, 1953), pp. 145–92. Includes almost half of Artaud's book: "Preface: The Theater and Culture," "Staging and Metaphysics," "On the Balinese Theater," "Let's Have Done with Masterpieces," "The Theater of Cruelty (First Manifesto)," "The Theater of Cruelty (Second Manifesto)."

―――. "General Security—The Liquidation of Opium." Translated by L. Dejardin, in Philip Lamantia, *Narcotica* ["I demand extinction of laws prohibiting narcotic drugs"] (San Francisco: Auerhahn Press, 1959), n.p.

―――. "A Letter to the Legislator of the Law on Narcotics." Translated by L. Dejardin (?), in Philip Lamantia, *Narcotica* ["I demand extinction of the laws prohibiting narcotic drugs"] (San Francisco: Auerhahn Press, 1959), n.p.

―――. "[Letter] To Louis Jouvet." Translated by V. Corti, *Tulane Drama Review* 9, no. 3 (Spring, 1965): 87–89.

―――. "Letters from Rodez." Translated by E. S. Seldon, *Evergreen Review* 4, no. 11 (January–February, 1960): 60–84.

―――. "No More Masterpieces." Translated by M. C. Richards, *Evergreen Review* 2, no. 5 (Summer, 1958): 150–59. Reprinted in *Writers in Revolt,* edited by T. Southern, R. Seaver, and A. Trocchi (New York: Berkeley Publishing Corporation, 1965), pp. 101–8. Also reprinted in *The Theater and Its Double* (see below).

―――. "The Philosophers' Stone: A Mime Play." Translated by V. Corti, *Tulane Drama Review* 9, no. 3 (Spring, 1965): 89–94.

―――. [Poem beginning: "It isn't possible that in the end the miracle may not occur . . ."], *Origin: A Quarterly for the Creative,* no. 11 (Autumn, 1953), p. 131.

―――. "Scenarios and Arguments." Translated by V. Corti and S. Sanzenbach, *Tulane Drama Review* 11 no. 1 (Fall, 1966): 166–85. Consists of English translations of the following film scenarios and notes on the film: "Questions and Answers," "Eighteen Seconds," "Two Nations on the Outer Edge of Mongolia," "Cinema and Abstraction," "The Shell and the Clergyman," "Motion Pictures and Witchcraft," "The Revolt of the Butcher," and "The Premature Senility of Film."

173

Artaud, Antonin. "Second-Class Humanity," *Origin: A Quarterly for the Creative,* no. 11 (Autumn, 1953), pp. 193–94.

Artaud, [Antonin]. ["Seven Short Poems"]. Translated by K. Rexroth, *The Black Mountain Review* 1, no. 2 (Summer, 1954): 8–11.

Artaud, Antonin. "Spurt of Blood." Translated by L. Ferlinghetti, *Evergreen Review* 7, no. 28 (January–February, 1963): 62–66.

―――. "States of Mind: 1921–1945." Translated by R. Cohn, *Tulane Drama Review* 8, no. 2 (Winter, 1963): 30–73. Consists of English translations of letters and excerpts under the following titles: "Letter to Max Jacob (1921)," "To Mlle. Yvonne Gilles (1921)," "The Atelier of Charles Dullin (1921)," "The Theatre of the Atelier (1922)," "From *The Umbilicus of Limbo* (1924)," "The Spurt of Blood (1924)," "To the Director of the Comédie Française (1925)," "The Alfred Jarry Theatre (1926)," "Manifesto for a Theatre-Abortion (1926)," "To Jean Paulhan (1927)," "To Abel Gance (1927)," "Production Plan for Strindberg's *Ghost Sonata* (1928?)," "The Evolution of Scenery (1928?)," "To Louis Jouvet (1931)," "Declaration (1931)," "[Four Letters] To Louis Jouvet (1931)," "To Jean Paulhan (1932)," "About a Lost Play (1934)," and "To Henri Parisot (1945)" (this last letter translated by V. Corti).

―――. "Symbolic Mountains." Transalted by V. Corti, *Tulane Drama Review* 9, no. 3 (Spring, 1965): 94–98.

―――. *The Theater and Its Double.* Translated by M. C. Richards. New York: Grove Press, 1958.

―――. "There's an Old Story." Translated by D. Rattray, *City Lights Journal,* no. 1 (1963), pp. 104–6.

―――. "Three Letters by Antonin Artaud." Translated by T. Fitzsimmons, *Evergreen Review* 7, no. 28 (January–February, 1963): 52–61.

―――. "To End God's Judgment." Translated and introduced by V. Corti, *Tulane Drama Review* 9, no. 3 (Spring, 1965): 56–87.

―――. "To Have Done with the Judgment of God." Translated

by G. Wernham, *Northwest Review* 6, no. 4 (Fall, 1963):
45–72.

———. "The Tree." Translated by P. Zweig, *Chelsea*, no. 13
["Special French Issue"] (June, 1963), p. 20.

[Artaud, Antonin]. "Van Gogh: The Man Suicided by Society,"
[translated by B. Frechtman], *The Tiger's Eye*, no. 7 (March,
1949), pp. 93–115. Author's and translator's name appear only
in table of contents. Reprinted in *The Trembling Lamb* (with
texts by LeRoi Jones and Carl Solomon) (New York: John
Fles—Editor, n.d. [1959?]), pp. 2–23.

# INDEX

187